My Life as a Hooker

MY LIFE AS A HOOKER

Summersdale Publishers Ltd
46 West Street
Chichester
West Sussex
PO19 1RP
UK

www.summersdale.com

Printed and bound in Great Britain

ISBN: 978-1-84953-211-2

Substantial discounts on bulk quantities of Summersdale books are available to corporations, professional associations and other organisations. For details telephone Summersdale Publishers on (+44-1243-771107), fax (+44-1243-786300) or email (nicky@summersdale.com).

My Life as a
Hooker

When a Middle-Aged Bloke
Discovered Rugby

Steven Gauge

summersdale

Contents

Chapter 1

Little Legs

Oxford psychology professor the late Michael Argyle said that the happiest people in the world were those who were either active members of a religious group or those who took part in team sports. So it was that at the age of thirty-five, as a miserable atheist, I took up playing rugby.

I hadn't played any rugby since I was about thirteen at school in Wimbledon. Even then I hadn't really played very much at all. For several years I convinced the rowing teachers that I was playing rugby, whilst convincing the rugby teachers that I was doing rowing. Meanwhile I went home and did very little indeed.

If you are no use at sport as a child you will be cruelly mocked and ridiculed. Those who are not particularly well co-ordinated and have thin skins will eventually give up and go away to find some other activity, like shoplifting or solvent abuse. However, when you take up a team sport like rugby as an adult, even if you have absolutely no idea what you are doing, no one gives you a hard time. People are just pathetically grateful that you have turned up. They are nice to you because you have made up the numbers so that they can have a proper game. If you add to that a willingness to play in the front row, they can have contested scrums and you will have made some friends for life.

Rugby seemed to be a great place to deal with my own personal midlife crisis. I was in a relatively senior job in a large chamber of commerce and government-funded business support operation. Having spent the earlier part of my career in a more metrosexual media and political environment, I was now surrounded by some very blokey blokes; they were all either go-getting entrepreneurial types, or failed businessmen who had become business advisers. Most seemed to spend their days talking about sport and cars. If I was going to get on with this crowd, as the saying goes, I needed to 'man up'.

I had also recently acquired contact lenses after a lifetime in glasses in a bout of midlife vanity. It could have been worse: others of my generation were bleaching their hair, getting inappropriate piercings and wearing leather trousers. Contact lenses paved the way to contact sports.

So when I found my way to Warlingham Rugby Club, I was delighted to discover a home for a group of men, all enjoying their own particular mid, early or later life crises and having a good time into the bargain. Here, by a Surrey playing field in the late summer, I found my way to the changing rooms and pulled on my newly purchased boots.

Warlingham is like many rugby clubs in the UK. There is a nice enough clubhouse with a huge function room, a cosy bar and some basic, bare-brick changing rooms. It prides itself on being one of the few clubs with a huge traditional communal bath. It has five pitches and shares the premises with a netball team and a cricket club. Every now and again someone will apply for some lottery money, send out an appeal or send off an insurance claim and a few improvements or repairs will be done by someone's mate.

There is a floodlit training pitch and on a Tuesday and Thursday evening throughout the autumn, winter and spring, men of various shapes and sizes turn up for training.

It's only when you look at the car park on a training night that you realise the wide range of people that get involved. One of the joys of amateur club rugby is the diversity of the sorts of people who play. From city boys who turn up in suits and smart cars, to builders and landscape gardeners who turn up in battered Ford Transit vans, once everyone is changed and on the pitch your background is almost irrelevant. Traditional British social divisions are replaced by a far more sinister and uncrossable barrier, rugby's very own apartheid: the distinction between forwards and backs.

That was the first tricky decision I had to make at my first training session. After a bit of running around to warm up we were told to divide up into forwards and backs. Which was I? I had absolutely no idea, and no time to decide. As far as I could tell, from watching the odd international on the TV, the forwards seemed to have to do a lot of fairly technical stuff: scrums, line-outs, rucks, mauls, ear-biting, eye-gouging etc. These were dark arts of which I knew nothing. The backs seemed to have a fairly straightforward job of standing in a line, throwing the ball to each other and running a bit. How hard could that be? I decided to be a back.

The coach for that evening was a nice bloke called Neil Farmer, a ponytailed schoolteacher (pottery, I guessed), tall and thin with a good line in sarcasm. He took one look at me as I jogged off to join the backs and, with his eyebrows making a bid for freedom off the top of his head, said, 'Are you sure?'

I'm not a hugely tall person and the modest belly that I carry around with me for comfort and protection is ever so slightly out of proportion with my height. The coach, as might anyone else, looked at me and saw an overweight hobbit who ought to be in the front row, if anywhere at all.

However, I stuck with the backs for the first session. A seventeen-year-old with enormous patience told me where to stand, when to run and what to do if I caught the ball. We ran around a bit and passed the ball to each other. In the words of Aleksandr the Meerkat, 'Simples.'

One of the things that have impressed me about club rugby is that I can't think of many other situations where a middle-aged fat bloke can interact socially with hoody-wearing teenagers. Probably the only other time it happens is when you're being mugged. Talking to teenagers is normally unbearably painful. Add a rugby ball into the equation, however, and suddenly it seems to work. It turns out that they can actually be quite pleasant. The young man who looked after me at my first session on the playing fields of Warlingham Rugby Club did a great job and I've never looked back.

I did quickly realise, however, that I was never going to be a back. There really was an awful lot of running around involved. An independent assessment of my physique by the third-team captain, Mark O'Connor, suggested that I was the perfect stature to become a hooker. That's the chap in the middle of the front row of the scrum who has the job of hooking back the ball with his foot, so that it pops out of the back of the scrum into the grateful hands of the scrum half.

I was delighted that my potential had been spotted so early – that someone had singled me out for this important and highly technical position. Little did I realise that Mark O'Connor, like every other club captain in every other club, would have the unenviable job of finding at least three people, week in week out, prepared to risk their necks in the middle of the scrum. Surrey physiotherapists were rubbing their cash registers with glee as another poor misguided fool volunteered for the front row.

As it turned out, hooking was a great job for me as someone completely new to the game who didn't really know what was going on elsewhere on the pitch. I had two clear tasks and both of them were part of restarting the game. I had to throw the ball in at the line-out and hook the ball back in the scrum. The rest of the game was far too chaotic and complicated for me at that stage, and much of it still is.

As a hooker, I wasn't going to have too many decisions to make about where to go and what to do. I could generally run around, keeping close enough to the play to look as if I was involved, whilst remaining just far enough away to avoid getting hurt. Then when the game stopped the referee would either call for a scrum or a line-out and then I had one or other of my two jobs to do.

So my position was sorted. I was beginning to feel ready for a proper game.

It was never entirely clear how the actual games got organised. Senior-looking players were always very vague about when games would happen, who they would be with and what side would be playing. For a while it seemed that they were waiting for some proper players to emerge from somewhere, possibly when the cricket season ended, or the ground got softer, or Jupiter moved out of alignment with Saturn. There was talk of 4th sides, 5th sides, the As, the Extra As, the Vets, the Development Squad. A fog of confusion was carefully created so I carried on turning up for training and waited for the call.

Eventually it came. Someone called Bill rang. He was organising a team and I needed to meet him and the rest of the team at Warlingham Clubhouse at about 12.30 on Saturday. I explained that I had never played before, didn't really understand the game and would need looking after, but I'd be happy to come on as a sub maybe for about ten minutes if that was all right. We agreed that would be fine and I invested in a pair of blue-and-white-striped club socks.

Saturday arrived and there I was, somewhat nervous at the clubhouse. Gradually it became apparent that efficiency and organisational prowess is not a common feature of rugby clubs. The apparently simple act of getting thirty players onto a rugby pitch is strewn with untold obstacles and pitfalls. After about an hour of waiting around, while a stressed and visibly balding middle-aged man made frantic phone calls, about a dozen of us got back into our cars and headed towards Battersea.

We sat in traffic for what seemed like an eternity and eventually made it to our opposition's clubhouse and got changed. At this point I was still fairly relaxed as I assumed that the rest of the team would be arriving at some point and I would be able to watch from the touchline, warm up for a bit and then come on as a supersub for the final ten minutes.

About three minutes before the kick-off, Bill the captain said to me, 'There's been a bit of a change of plan. Sorry and all that but you're starting and going to have to play a full game.' I gulped. This was it. There was a half-hearted team talk and suddenly I was playing.

I must have been terrible. I had no idea what I was doing. I got in the way, fell over and gave the ball away to the opposition. But no one complained or moaned at me. No one seemed to mind. Eventually the game settled into a sort of rhythm, tries were scored and conversions were kicked.

At one point I found myself with the ball. I've no idea how it happened. I was lurking around at the back of a maul, trying to keep out of the way, and someone thrust a ball into my stomach. With a huge dollop of beginner's luck I was off and running, having mysteriously got away from the pack of forwards before they'd noticed. I was going vaguely in the right direction, towards the opposition's try line, with a lifetime's supply of adrenalin pumping through my veins. As I recall it now, I ran for what felt like 40 or 50 yards. In reality it was probably more like 10 or 20. I ran for what felt like ages until two or three of the opposition headed towards me.

At this point I had no idea what to do. The only thing I had really learnt from the training was that you had to pass the ball backwards but I couldn't see anyone on my side anywhere near me. I was clearly about to be torn limb from limb by the opposition players coming towards me at speed. In that situation the ball could potentially go in any direction. I couldn't let the ball go forward. The only thing I could think of to do was throw the ball in a great loop over my head, in the hope that someone on my side would catch it and everyone else would leave me alone.

No one caught the ball and I got splattered anyway. The opposition picked up the ball and ran all the way back up the pitch. I was later fined a fiver for my random act of jettisoning the ball by the captain in the pub as he sought to raise funds for another round of drinks. It was an inauspicious debut but I was still quite chuffed to have done the William Webb-Ellis thing of picking up the ball and running with it for a bit. I was even more chuffed that the huge opposition prop referred to me as 'Little legs' throughout the rest of the game.

Over the last few years I have tried to recapture the adrenalin rush of that first match and that first run with the ball. Moments like it have been rare, but along the way I have met some great people and had some great experiences. I even rose to the dizzy heights of captain of Warlingham 4th XV and helped to steer it from being the third-worst side in the county to being the Surrey Foundation League Champions.

I have discovered a wonderful game, far removed from the professional televised glamour of international rugby, where ordinary blokes with ordinary jobs (and some extraordinary bellies) get together once in a while and have a great time rolling around in the mud. I hope to share some of the sheer joy of the sport that is amateur club rugby with you in the following chapters.

Chapter 2

Training: Not for the Faint-hearted

There is still something deep in the English sporting psyche that regards practising and training as something close to cheating. The true sporting gentleman should perform effortlessly without at any point being seen to try. However, my level of understanding of rugby was so low and my skills so remedial that I had to do something if I was to survive in my newfound sport.

I made every effort to get to training on a Tuesday and Thursday evening as often as I could. Rushing back from work and changing from my suit into odd bits of ill-fitting sportswear, I got myself onto the training pitch and tried to fathom out how the game was supposed to be played.

Although Warlingham was and is a warm and welcoming club, there was something painful and embarrassing about turning up to training when I really didn't have the faintest idea what I was doing. As players arrive on the training pitch, the first thing they do is stand around gently throwing the ball to each other. That looked relatively straightforward. I've been able to throw a ball since I was a toddler. I could join in with that. What could be simpler?

Quite a lot, it turns out. As I joined the circle it became apparent that I couldn't even manage to pass to someone standing a few feet away. Each time I attempted to throw the ball to someone, it would tumble through the air and fall short. Everyone else could, with a clever flick of the wrist, make it spin on its axis and glide aerodynamically to the next person. I desperately required special needs one-to-one tuition.

I have a much younger brother called Nathan who is my parents' somewhat more successful attempt at producing a son and heir. Although we are roughly the same size, Nathan is a much better shape and eighteen years younger. He appeared on the scene just as I had left home for university. Years of intensive competitive gymnastics and first-team school rugby have put muscles on him in all the right places. He is a delightful, mild-mannered chap but hidden reserves of testosterone have given him the ability to turn on impressive levels of aggression on the pitch.

So it was to my little brother Nathan that I turned for some beginner's tuition. He patiently took me through the basics of the game in our parents' back garden, teaching me how to throw the ball and roughly what I should do if I ever caught it.

'If you do get the ball, just hold onto it and run forwards as far as you can until someone stops you,' he said. Sensible and delightfully simple advice, I thought.

This was all of course embarrassingly up the wrong way. It should have been me, in my role as an older brother, teaching him. There was such a big age gap that we hadn't really grown up together. I'd missed the opportunity to practise the skills I would need for tackling people on a rugby pitch by gently beating him up whilst our parents weren't looking. Instead Nathan was now patiently and painstakingly taking a dozy middle-aged man though the fundamentals of the game he had learnt at the age of eleven.

'Erm… what about this tackling malarkey?' I asked.

Apparently all I needed to do was get low and use my shoulder. Given I am already fairly low down to start with, this all seemed fairly doable.

Nathan took me through it at a walking pace. It was easy enough to get my arms round his thighs as he allowed me to stop him and pull him to the ground but it was all a little bit odd. He tried jogging towards me with the ball but that became a little more complicated as I struggled to work out which bit of me to put where. Nathan, who is training to be a doctor, at this stage began assessing me to see if there were any other symptoms of emerging mental illness. He began to wonder what on earth could be driving someone he had previously looked up to and respected to take up a sport so clearly unsuited to his physique, fitness and general cack-handedness. Before he decided to have me sectioned, I thought we had better call it a day. I was going to have to take my chances against real opposition.

It had been a very gentle introduction to the art of tackling. When I got back onto the Warlingham training pitch I was to discover quite how much pain could be involved in that particular aspect of the game.

One of the training drills used to develop tackling skills is known as a 'one-on-one'. A rectangular strip of the pitch is marked out with little cones. On the coach's signal, two players run to opposite ends of the strip. One of them then picks up a ball and tries to run to the far end past the other player who tries his best to stop him. One evening our coach, Neil Farmer (ponytail, teacher, possibly pottery), thought this would be a good idea and got us to line up in twos.

There was a little buzz of excitement as the players moved into position. The banter and the bravado went up a notch. A few scores were about to be settled, I suspected, as people prepared to stake their claim for selection in the first team on the strength of their tackling prowess.

As with most training exercises, my strategy was to drift around at the back of the crowd, watching the first few keen beans demonstrate what we were supposed to be doing. Pairs of players in front of me split up, ran round opposite ends of the cones and then met in the middle. A shimmy here, a tackle there. It all looked relatively straightforward. Some of the tackles looked quite hard but everyone seemed to emerge reasonably unscathed. As I got to the front of the queue, I was paired with someone called Kieron, a shaven-headed prop, who, to be honest, didn't look terribly fast.

The coach gave the signal and I ran to my left, around the cone and collected the ball. Then instantly, out of nowhere, a bald head accompanied by a very hard shoulder bone and powered by 18 stone of muscle crashed into my midriff with a thud. I hit the ground like a dollop of wet Christmas pudding mix and faintly heard a congratulatory cheer from the watching players.

After a little while, I realised that I couldn't actually breathe at all. I felt like I had had all the air knocked out of my lungs and there was no way they were going to be persuaded to inhale ever again. Collapsed in a heap on the floor, I made a few groaning noises as I struggled to get some air. I wondered vaguely whether this would be how it all ended. I'd had a reasonable innings, I supposed; married, a couple of nice children, some interesting jobs and some good friends. I hadn't really made my mark on the world yet, though, and it seemed a shame that it would all end on a cold wet rugby pitch, in the arms of a pottery teacher with a ponytail.

Neil tried to get me breathing again by lifting my shoulders up with his arms under my armpits, and Lacey, the club physiotherapist, made reassuring noises. Slowly, after what seemed like an age, in small, shallow gasps, I started breathing again. I wasn't going to die just yet, but I also wasn't going to be doing one-on-one tackling drills with the first-team front row again in a hurry.

At the lower levels of the game, the training pitch would appear to be a much more hazardous place than the game itself. Midweek sessions see workplace frustrations and bitter internal club rivalries worked out with brutal regularity. Competitive leagues normally sort players into roughly the same levels of ability. Club training sessions routinely pit pumped-up 1st-team adrenalin junkies against unfit novices trying to learn the game or rusty returners hoping to remember some of their moves. Over the last few years I have incurred far more injuries from training pitch mismatches and mishaps than I have ever encountered in competitive games against other clubs.

The most dangerous moment on the training pitch, however, is when someone suggests a 1st v 2nd team match. If you ever hear this suggestion, you should remember a very important appointment somewhere else and head straight to your car or bicycle, or failing that hide under a table in the committee room. A 1st v 2nd training match is far more deadly than any local derby and will inevitably end badly. The only reason such games are suggested in the first place is because a handful of players are disgruntled at having been left out of the 1st team and have something to prove. Bruised egos make for bad-tempered boys and even bigger bruises elsewhere.

As a novice I wasn't prepared for quite the level of animosity when I huddled in with the second string for a pre-match team talk before my inaugural 1st v 2nd contest. I thought we were all friends here and although we were on different sides we were still members of the same club. I couldn't have been more wrong. A young barrister and aspiring local politician was firing up his fellow 1st-team rejects using his best courtroom oratory skills and he was not best pleased. Cruelly overlooked for a 1st-team place, he was very clear that this was to be a serious competitive game and he was looking for our support as he asserted his 1st-team claim.

The coach had decided to play with the 1st team in order to make up the numbers, and after about ten minutes of intensive rugby found himself at the bottom of a ruck in close proximity to our young barrister. No one really knows for sure what happened next but as the ruck broke up, the barrister emerged with a cheeky grin, followed by a very angry-looking coach, who then proceeded to chase him around the pitch, screaming and swearing until someone held him back. The barrister never made it back into the 1st team after that but felt, somehow, that he had made his point.

Fortunately, in between the training field bust-ups and breakdowns, some more useful lessons were learnt. Generous and patient coaches and fellow players taught me the finer points of being a hooker; how to angle my body in the scrum and signal to the scrum half so that I could time my strike for the ball perfectly and win scrums where my side had the put-in. I was taught how to arch my back, which had spent far too many years hunched over a computer keyboard, to launch a decent line-out throw. If at any point the drills began to look a bit too violent for my liking I would toddle off to the try line and practise getting my line-out throws in a straight line and at the perfect height by aiming for a little strip of gaffer tape on the goalposts.

Patience seemed to me to be the greatest virtue of the club. I was always amazed at how tolerant and indulgent all the coaches were as I fumbled and dropped my way through every training session.

Warlingham is a club which seems to get through at least two head coaches every season. The stresses of this job are many and might explain the high turnover. First a coach has to find something to do for between twenty and forty agitated and frustrated young men for one or two evenings a week. These are the keen ones, who are desperate for the status and recognition of winning a place in the 1st team and make up the bulk of the players at training. The few middle-aged ones like me are happy to jog around the periphery of the training field and are very easily pleased. A selection of drills and exercises need to be organised that are interesting and challenging enough to keep everyone entertained but simple enough to be understood by your average front row.

Coaches have to cajole and encourage as many people as possible to come up and train and then find ways to keep them all involved as they then fail to make it into the 1st team. They have to be impartial selectors even though the only reason they got involved in coaching in the first place was to support and encourage their own offspring. They have to compete for the time and attention of the fittest and most naturally imposing young men in the area.

Every Saturday afternoon, coaches then proceed to pump their charges full of confidence, adrenalin, testosterone and alcohol in roughly equal measures on and around the pitch, before unleashing them on the nearest pubs and clubs in the evening. The following week, they have to extract the players from the hangover, hospital or police cell they ended up in and start the process all over again. Little wonder so few last the season.

The other problem is that most coaches are former players. They may have been good players, in which case the skills that may have made them great on the pitch – aggression, brute force and easy recourse to violence – tend not to make them all that good at the more subtle art of coaching. Alternatively, they were poor players, with little clue about the game, but keen to cling on and around the sport in some way or another. These coaches often are better communicators, talking a good talk. They may get away with the job for a few weeks, but eventually the senior players begin to realise that there is little or no substance behind their fine words. Gradually their position is undermined, they are ignored and the players return to beating each other up at training to pass the time.

The best coaches have to have played at a sufficiently high level to command respect but have retained sufficient brain cells to be able to communicate in words of more than one syllable. One of the best I encountered at Warlingham was Nick Robinson, not the BBC Political Editor but someone who had played rugby at a reasonably senior level for some years but managed to extract himself from the game soon enough to have kept most of his mental faculties intact.

Robbo, as he was known, managed to retain a level of respect and affection from the senior players by playing alongside them every now and again to show that he still 'had it' and drinking them all under the table with alarming regularity. With me he showed the sort of patience and understanding that is normally reserved for primary school children being taught to read or little old ladies trying to master the use of the Internet.

At my first few training sessions, when I really did not have a clue, Robbo somehow managed to find something I had done to be positive about and keep me turning up. ('Well done there, you remembered to pass the ball backwards that time.') Most coaches adopt a straightforward and instinctive approach of insults and obscenities to get their point across. Robbo was a rare exception.

Games of touch rugby, where the more violent elements of the game are removed, allowed me to get a bit fitter and learn how and where to position myself on the pitch. Pacing myself carefully, I very occasionally managed to catch a pass and run a bit. Following Nathan's advice, I would just put my head down and run forwards in a straight line until somebody stopped me. That seemed to be vaguely useful taking my side up the pitch a few yards. I could leave the younger and fitter ones to make all the fancy sidesteps, switch-passes and try-scoring breaks.

And then it happened. I caught a ball and simultaneously found a gap in between two players who at that precise moment were fractionally more out of breath than I was. Seeing the opportunity, my little legs seemed to gain a little burst of speed and I was through, running towards the try line with a clear view and the ball in my hand. There was a cry from behind me of 'Go on, Gaugey,' and I could see someone out of the corner of my eye running to try and catch me. But I was already far enough ahead and got over the try line just in time. Scoring my first try, albeit in a game of touch, was a simple but enormously satisfying pleasure. It made me realise that this was clearly a far better way to spend a midweek evening than vegetating in front of a soap opera on the TV. I was pathetically happy with this minor triumph. As I jogged back to join the rest of my team, I got a bit carried away and went to high-five Dave Halliwell, a rather tall second-row player – before realising I might have to stand on a chair to make contact.

Chapter 3

Crunch! Learning the Game by Trial but Mostly Error

One of the highlights of every season in the lower sides at Warlingham is a trip to Mitcham. Residents of this south London suburb would probably forgive me for pointing out that Mitcham has successfully managed to resist most attempts at gentrification and economic regeneration. It does have a cricket green and a pretty little windmill but it also has more than its fair share of social housing, and quite a few pound shops and cash converters. Its rugby club reflects the values of its local community. It is hard, down to earth and, as social reformers might say, it suffers from not having a level playing field. The rugby pitch is pretty uneven too, being on a recreation ground open to the Mitcham public, their dogs and the occasional joyrider, twenty-four hours a day.

Games between Mitcham and leafy, suburban Warlingham always have a certain edge. This may be something to do with the socio-economic and demographic disparity between the two communities. Warlingham is just outside the Greater London area and home to wealthy commuters. Warlingham has a village green, a Women's Institute and a Parish Council. For these and many other reasons there is always a massive fight halfway through the game between the two clubs.

But as this was one of my first games I was unaware of the treat I had in store.

At this stage in my rugby career I was still very hazy indeed about the game and what I was supposed to do with myself at any point other than in a scrum or a line-out. At my level of the game there is an awful lot of something that is called 'loose play'. This is where the ball is generally bouncing around and the forwards are running around like headless chickens, bumping into each other, falling over and lunging or hacking at the ball.

Being a man, I couldn't possibly consider asking anyone what I was supposed to do or what any of the rules were, just as I wouldn't possibly imagine ever asking for directions when driving. No doubt the rules would eventually become apparent and I would pick things up as I went along.

It turns out there is some regulation about not touching the ball with your hand when you and/or it are on the ground during a ruck. I didn't really know for certain what technically constituted a ruck at this point (actually I'm still not a hundred per cent sure).

All I really knew was that it was good for someone on your team to have the ball and there was this thing about passing the ball backwards.

The reason I now know this rule about not handling the ball on the ground is not because I have carefully studied the RFU rules book as amended by the International Rugby Board experimental laws implementation subcommittee. Nor is it because a patient coach, captain or referee took me to one side to explain the technical aspects of the game and my role. The only reason that I now know this rule is because early in the game against Mitcham I happened to find myself lying in the recreation field mud right next to the ball and an assortment of other legs, arms and torsos. With what I thought at the time was remarkably quick thinking, I recognised that there were more of my team behind me and lots of the opposition in front of me on the pitch. The simplest and most efficient thing to do all round, I thought, would be to push the ball, with my hand, back towards our players and away from theirs.

Big mistake.

At this point I heard an unequivocal south London instruction: 'STAMP ON 'IS FAAHKIN 'AND!'

Immediately a boot or, more precisely, four rounded metal studs attached to a boot, descended and proceeded to grind their way between my knuckles and metacarpals. The pain at the time was excruciating and a bit of a shock for me as a mild-mannered man who had managed to make it to middle age without ever having been in anything resembling a physical altercation. However, as we say in the corporate executive training world, the 'Learning

Point' here was that handling the ball on the ground can lead to handling difficulties later, so it's probably best not to do it when anyone can see what you are doing. As a result of one well-placed boot I was immediately fully apprised of the basic regulation concerning handling the ball in the ruck. I've not needed to double-check it in the rule book subsequently and haven't broken that rule since.

There are a few other rules about the game that one gradually absorbs by osmosis but a less than comprehensive understanding of them all need not be a barrier to the enjoyment of the game at the lower level. In more serious sides, in the upper echelons of the game, knowledge of the rules is only useful if you are also fully aware of how and when to break them. Rigid adherence to the regulations at a senior level is, I'm told, the way to certain defeat. Playing the referee is the key to success for the serious player.

At the raw grass-roots level the average player can generally pick up the gist of the game over the course of eighty minutes of being shouted at by the twenty-nine other players on the pitch. To avoid being offside one generally needs to be behind the ball or behind the rear foot of any scrum, ruck or maul. This is best achieved by not running around too enthusiastically at any point and not joining anything that looks like it might be a scrum, ruck or maul. Generally standing around watching the play from a safe distance is the best way to avoid falling foul and there will usually be some player somewhere gesticulating at you to get out of the way if you are in danger of infringing the rules.

There is apparently another rule about not holding on to the ball after you are tackled and have fallen to the ground, but at a beginner's level this is hardly worth worrying about. In the unlikely event that you get the ball and hang on to it long enough to be tackled then your chances of keeping a grip on it are pretty minimal. The ball will probably slip out of your grasp as you put your hands and arms to the much more important task of breaking your fall and protecting your head and vital organs from other people's boots. If by some fluke you are still hanging on to the ball as you land in the mud, there will be plenty of other people trying to rip it from you. They will probably succeed, as they will be stronger than you. All you can do is hope that the first person to get it is one of your own teammates.

Once you are on the ground it is probably sensible to stay there for a little while, catch your breath and wait for the play to move a safe distance away before getting to your feet. Then you can pass the time by seeing if you can predict where the next scrum or line-out will be and gently jog into your position for the restart. This will make it more likely that you don't break any rules or bones over the course of the rest of the game.

There is one other rule of rugby that I learnt the hard way. It turns out that you are not supposed to block or obstruct another player when neither of you has the ball. I discovered this in a very competitive game played against local rivals Purley John Fisher. It was towards the end of the season and I was beginning to get the hang of the game. I was getting a little bit fitter and was very occasionally making a useful contribution to the side.

Our club rivalry with Purley John Fisher seemed to go back a long way. John Fisher is a local Catholic school and derby games between us and them seem to degenerate into sectarian singing and occasional bar brawls. John Fisher Old Boys used to be Warlingham's next-door neighbours until they fell on hard times. Rather than merge with Warlingham they paired up with Purley, another side a few miles away, and the rivalry seems to have festered from there.

Matching up rugby sides is not an exact science and at the lower levels of the game you never really know what quality of side you are playing until after the referee blows his whistle for the kick-off. Clubs like Warlingham and PJF may claim to run three or four sides each week. However, it does not necessarily follow that if you are scheduled to play a third XV, two better sides from that club will be playing someone else. Where there is an important local derby, players may shuffle between sides to vent their own grudges and feuds. So it transpires that some games are a lot tougher than others.

This particular local derby was billed as a third-team fixture but it felt a lot tougher than that. Fortunately two of my favourite forwards, Phil Evans and Dave Halliwell, were playing in the second row behind me in the scrum.

The second row or locks have the delightful task of sticking their heads between the front row's backsides, their arms up between their legs, grabbing hold of anything they can find and generally holding the front row together. They tend to have tape round their ears, Vaseline all over their head and a slightly dazed and ashamed expression on their face.

This is one position that really highlights the difference between real rugby that is played on soggy, deserted pitches across the UK and the other version that is played on the television between professional sides. At the higher levels of rugby, second-row players are often the real powerhouses of a side. England's World Cup-winning captain Martin Johnson dominated games from his position in the second row. Usually the tallest players on the pitch, they are raised aloft in the line-out as they compete for the ball in the air.

However, in the lower leagues such as the Surrey Foundation, where the Warlingham 4th XV competes, the situation is somewhat different. No one ever really wants to play in the second row. It is normally a position allocated to the newest recruit or last person to arrive in the changing room and claim a shirt. The benefits are limited and the opportunities to shine are few.

The glamorous 'leaping salmon' job in the line-out is usually given to the lightest person on the pitch as it is all a bit of an effort to lift anyone weighing more than 11 stone. Lower-league second rows are limited to the ear-mangling, dirt-eating job of trying to stop the scrum from going backwards. It takes a particular sort of character to succeed at this level and Dave and Phil have plenty of character.

Phil Evans is a club veteran, and occasional professional Welshman, for whom a pre-match pint is an essential part of his warm-up routine. The sight of him with a cigarette in his mouth and half a tub of Vaseline smeared over his bald head is enough to send small children into years of therapy. Dave Halliwell, younger but even more substantial, has grown up with Warlingham Rugby. His father played for the club and they are both Northern ginger giants. Way too substantial to ever be lifted off the ground without the aid of an industrial crane or twin jet engine, he put his dreams of a modelling career behind him as he happily sacrificed his boyish good looks for the benefit of the club on more than one occasion.

With Phil and Dave pushing from behind in every scrum I was having a good afternoon in the pack and enjoying the game enormously. I was feeling reasonably fit and at one point the ball was kicked towards our try line and I began to run towards it. A rather tall opposition forward was also running quite enthusiastically alongside me. As the two of us raced to the ball I calculated that the odds were not stacked terribly well in my favour. If we both got to the ball together, the chances were that my opponent would have a better idea of what to do, would grab the ball and run off and score a try. My best hope was to slow him down a bit so that someone else from my side might turn up and take charge of the situation.

So nonchalantly, all innocent-like, I got in his way a bit, running alongside him but not quite in the same direction, pushing him away from where he was trying to get to. This felt to me quite daring and a little bit brave. I was asserting myself, all 5 ft 6 in. of me, on the pitch and making my presence felt. My opponent didn't seem to agree. All he could see was an almost certain try-scoring opportunity ahead of him and an annoying little hobbit getting in his way. He swore and lashed out, catching me with a fist or possibly the heel of his hand square in the nose. There was a crack and I fell to the floor in quite a bit of pain.

My face, hands, shirt and the grass around me seemed to be covered in blood. I was dazed and confused but managed to affect a sufficient degree of outrage and indignation to see my opponent sent off to the sin bin for ten minutes. Meanwhile, I went off to clean up and attempt to stem the flow of blood. This seemed to take quite a while but I was determined to get back on the pitch. We were short of players and there was no one to sub for me.

Eventually someone rummaged around in a first aid kit and found what can only be described as a couple of nasal tampons. These were stuffed up my nostrils and I got myself back on the pitch just in time for the next scrum – not a pretty sight for my opposing front row.

As my assailant came back on to the pitch, Dave Halliwell and Phil Evans informed me that they were very keen to welcome him back into the game with their own particular brand of restorative justice. The small matters of winning the ball or scoring any points were a long way down their list of priorities. Phil and Dave spent the rest of the game looking for any and every opportunity to clatter into his ribs, limbs and tender regions, within the rules of the game of course, until they had avenged the original assault. It would appear that I had acquired two rather splendid henchmen.

It took about a week for my nose to stop bleeding properly and I haven't really been able to breathe properly through my right nostril ever since. Strangely enough, though, I was quite pleased with myself. For the first time ever in a game of rugby I'd been playing well enough and being enough of a nuisance to warrant being thumped. It's normally only the better players that get hurt. Here I was nursing a quality injury, incurred in the line of duty. The last man in defence skilfully executing an heroic, if ever so slightly illegal, try-stopping manoeuvre.

I had cracked more than just my nose. I had cracked the game. I might not know all the rules or the tactics but I knew enough to irritate the opposition, stop them from scoring and get one of them sent off into the bargain. I had teammates prepared to go out and exact retribution for me. With the blood still dripping out of my nose, that post-match pint in the Purley John Fisher clubhouse bar was one of the sweetest I have ever drunk.

Chapter 4

Two Steps Forward, Thirteen Pints Back

Woody Allen was right when he declared that eighty per cent of success in life comes from just turning up. In my first few years as a more mature student of rugby, the secret of my success was an ability to read the club circular, get to the club on time and, if we were playing away, to make sure I knew where we were going. This gave me a distinct advantage over other players who might have been much better at rugby than me but couldn't organise themselves out from under a duvet on a Saturday morning.

The fact was that I was beginning to depend on my regular Saturday afternoon expeditions on a rugby pitch to keep me sane.

Life was getting complicated personally and professionally. I had two delightful children who were turning into slightly disorientating teenagers and I was struggling to cope with the additional pressure that had come with a promotion at work. I discovered that, no matter how stressed I was and how many complications I was mulling over in my mind, there was nothing that cleared the head better than a game of rugby. It is simply impossible to think about a difficult appraisal, a budget reforecast or another pointless PowerPoint presentation when a 6-foot, 20-stone prop is running at you with a rugby ball in one hand and a clenched fist in the other.

Actually I can still picture the player who helped me to realise the therapeutic power of rolling around on a rugby pitch in the mud with a load of fat blokes. A local side, Merton, had one particular prop who has helped to clear my mind at least twice a season. With a shaved head, a thickset muscular form and a slightly evil-looking goatee beard, he looks like Ming the Merciless on steroids. Locking horns with him in the front row for every scrum is unsettling enough, but once he gets the ball in his hand and a little speed on him, you really don't want to get in his way. The fear I felt coming up against him certainly did put petty office politics into perspective.

So, more and more I needed rugby and, fortunately, it needed me. A succession of captains of the lower Warlingham sides knew that when their preferred teenage front-row star couldn't be found anywhere after a Friday night out in Croydon, I would be at the clubhouse regardless, clutching a printed-out set of AA Route Map directions to whichever Surrey rugby club was playing host to us that weekend.

Captains are key figures in the success of any rugby club, but not necessarily for the reasons you might imagine. Apart from 1st-team captains of the larger clubs, the captain does not need to be the best player on the pitch. In fact being a decent player, or even thinking that you might be, is almost a positive disadvantage. If you are too good, better sides higher up the club will want you playing for them. The most important skill you need as a captain is the ability to operate a mobile phone and count to fifteen.

The captain's job at the level where most real club rugby is played is to somehow get fourteen other players to join him on the pitch in time for kick-off around 3 p.m. on a Saturday afternoon. This requires extensive use of a mobile phone for most of the preceding week. Texting, emailing and Facebook-stalking all also play a part in persuading twenty-eight reluctant feet into their rugby boots. Once they are on the pitch, the captain can relax until the game is over and it is time to collect the match subs.

Jason Urquart was an excellent captain in spite of having little recognisable skill on the pitch. As a forward, he had an alarming tendency to fly into a total panic whenever he was unfortunate enough to find the ball in his hands. Rather than doing anything as dangerous as running forward with the ball he would typically fling it backwards, vaguely in the direction of the nearest unsuspecting back, leaving them to be flattened by the opposition pack.

However, as a 3rd-team captain, Jason somehow managed to concoct a full team of players out of nowhere week after week. An insurance broker during the day, he used his easy charm to entice all sorts of players onto the pitch and at the same time keep the better ones from being noticed and then poached by the higher sides. Jason would always be the last to arrive for any games, mostly because he had spent the morning desperately phoning extra players or dragging hung-over teenagers out of their beds and into the clubhouse.

So in my late thirties, it gradually dawned on me that I had become Jason's regular hooker. It was an arrangement that worked well for a couple of seasons. He didn't need me to dress up in anything particularly risqué apart from a faded blue-and-white heavy cotton rugby shirt. He didn't need me to do anything too vulgar, other than cuddle in the middle of a field with him and thirteen other men on a Saturday afternoon.

With all this regular rugby, it was fairly difficult to avoid getting slightly fitter. I did begin to find that occasionally within a game I was up with the pace, getting into the general vicinity of the ball relatively quickly and beginning to make myself useful, mostly in the pushing and shoving department.

The most fun on the rugby pitch is probably to be had in a maul. This is where one player has the ball, is tackled but manages to stay on his feet. Other players from both teams gather round and attempt to either get the ball or prevent their opponents from doing so. The side with the ball also attempts to move the maul up the pitch, draining their opposing pack's energy and enthusiasm.

Once in a while I was able to get my head and shoulders into roughly the right position to shove my teammates towards the opposition try line. More often than not I would be hanging on for dear life, trying not to lose an arm, contact lens or item of clothing in the process. This aspect of the game is classic forwards play and on a wet and windy rugby pitch it is the perfect way to keep warm.

In midwinter games of low to middling rugby, on muddy pitches, the backs are generally left out quite a lot. In these conditions, forwards are more likely to keep the ball to themselves rather than risk passing a wet and slippery ball to freezing backs who have lost all sensation in their extremities.

On soggy wet days it was always good to be around Big Tony, who as the name suggests was and is a substantial prop. Tony came from possibly the wrong side of Croydon and his recreational and entrepreneurial pharmaceutical activities found him on the wrong side of the law at various points over a chequered career. I understand he spent a little time pleasuring Her Majesty and turned up to a few games sporting a curfew-monitoring ankle bracelet or 'Peckham Rolex' under his rugby socks.

However, with the help and support of many at the rugby club, Tony turned his life around and even became 1st-team captain for a bit. Tony is the only player I have actually seen stuff a rugby ball up his jumper in a maul to prevent the opposition from getting it, as we pushed his substantial weight deeper into our opponents' half.

As I got fitter and faster I was able to add a new trick to my game – support play. Again this doesn't require any great skill but looks good and keeps you close to the action. When I found myself with enough energy I would merrily chase alongside my teammates who had the ball so that if they got tackled, tired or just bored they could pop the ball to me. Sadly, most people knew of my lack of ability and unreliable hands and so even if they were stopped they would think twice – or possibly three or four times – before passing the ball to me.

Undeterred, I would keep running around after better players, like a pilotfish following a shark, in the hope that I would pick up some scraps. Time after time I would go off on pointless lung-busting runs, only to see someone tackled and lose the ball rather than give it to me. But eventually, on one afternoon, it was a tactic that would pay off.

Captain Urquart had put together an excellent side for a home fixture, packed with ringers from higher sides and former 1st-team players back from retirement for a fun afternoon. We were several points ahead and one particular tall dashing back had already picked up two tries with relative ease. We were edging towards the end of the game, with the result in little doubt and most players on both sides were thinking about their first post-match pint, rather than paying attention to anything on the pitch.

I, however, was feeling fit and thinking about the possibility of getting my first ever try after two or three seasons without troubling the scorekeeper. Suddenly, like a shot, our tall dashing back dashed off with the ball and I dashed after him. I managed somehow to stay within a couple of metres of him as he weaved past defender after demoralised defender. Unfortunately none of the opposition bothered to tackle him as they had already given up all hope of winning. So it looked like he would score yet another glorious try and retire to the bar to celebrate a hat-trick.

As he got over the try line, free of all opposition, he slowed down, turned round and looked back towards his teammates. By this point, with my excess baggage and belly, I had built up quite a bit of momentum and was finding slowing down a little more difficult. Possibly shocked by the sight of a wheezing overweight dwarf filling his field of vision, Dashing Back generously popped up an easy gentle pass to me, which I gratefully accepted, and then placed the ball onto the ground for my first ever try.

OK, so it was a bit of a charity try, given as a reward for effort and enthusiasm rather than ability, but my relentless running around had finally got me noticed and got me onto the scoresheet. It took a while to wipe the smile off my face. Once again rough-and-ready rugby at the weekend had cleared my head and given me the confidence and inner calm to cope with whatever life was going to throw at me.

Back in the clubhouse after the game, I bought a jug of beer for the team to celebrate scoring my first points for the club. Buying beer by the jug and consuming it by the barrel is all part and parcel of rugby at the amateur, social level. Beer and rugby are intricately linked, possibly more than any other sport. Although it was always possible to slip away quietly from the club after one or two post-match pints, pleading drink-driving laws and family commitments, it was always more fun when I managed to stay for a third, fourth and fifth pint and a few random shots of chilli vodka.

For the younger players in the club, post-match drinking was usually a warm-up for a taxi to Croydon and a boogie in whichever nightclub they hadn't been banned from yet. For the older players it was and remains the best sanctuary from tedious Saturday evening TV talent shows and celebrity pap. A quiet pint followed by several noisy ones in the safety and security of the clubhouse also seemed to be a good way to clear the mind, at least at the time. Sometimes it was a little too good at clearing the mind and left vast chunks of a Saturday evening unrecollectable.

Only once or twice did I venture out towards the dodgier parts of south London with the boys. When team spirit and camaraderie reached a certain level, it was agreed that we would go for a mid-season 3rd-team night out in Clapham. It started with a serious post-match warm-up in the clubhouse, with awards and drinking fines being dished out in roughly equal measure.

'The award for Most Improved Player goes to...' Jason paused for dramatic effect.

'Steven Gauge.'

He handed over a lump of faux marble with a bit of metal moulded into the shape of a rugby player clearly in much better condition than me. I think, to be absolutely honest, the award reflected the very low base that I started from rather than the heights I had obtained.

To celebrate, I was then required to drink a shot of chilli vodka, a drink created for no other purpose as far as I can tell, than to cause pain during the evening and the following morning.

We hopped into taxis to East Croydon station, where I seem to recall we picked up a bottle or two of port for the journey. We then drank our way to Clapham Junction and from bar to bar until we reached the legendary south London dance establishment that is Infernos. We sent our winger Steven Parker to the front of the queue, mostly because he had the best shoes, a bold-statement pair of gleaming white loafers, and we were swiftly ushered in.

I hadn't been anywhere like this for about twenty years, so it was all a bit of a shock to the system: dark, loud and heaving with good-looking girls and beery, lecherous boys. Young Steven Parker's white loafers appeared to have mystical pulling powers and he was soon whisked away by a lady of a certain age to her nearby flat not to be seen for the rest of the season. I danced wildly, enthusiastically and deeply inappropriately with a succession of terrified-looking young women until I did some basic maths and realised they were all at most half my age and not much older than my daughter. I made my excuses and left.

Fortunately, our tall, intimidating and conveniently sober winger Audley was on hand to escort me through the nocturnal nightmare of public transport in south London and somehow got me home, not before I had made a bit of a mess of the underpass at South Norwood railway station. It took the best part of a week to recover from the hangover and a little longer to recover my dignity and self-respect.

Chapter 5

Collateral Damage and a Cunning Plan

Things were going well for Warlingham 1st team and they had managed to get themselves promoted. The knock-on effect on the third team, however, was not altogether welcome. With the 1st team going up a league, the Surrey Rugby committee that organises the lower leagues decided that the lower Warlingham teams also needed to go up a league. They presumably reasoned that, as the 1st team had significantly improved, the lower sides in the club would inevitably become stronger too. Perhaps they thought we would absorb new skills and strength by osmosis, from sharing the occasional team bath.

Sadly the reverse was the case. With the 1st-team squad on fire, the already limited numbers of 3rd-team players who would dare to make an appearance at training dwindled drastically. There was little to be gained other than broken bones and strained self-esteem.

Although the 1st team was attracting new players, few of the old guard wanted to drop down to the lower sides. With their egos shattered, they suddenly discovered wives and girlfriends they didn't know they'd had. DIY projects and family social events became more attractive than swallowing their pride and playing in one of the lesser sides at the club.

So as the 1st team went up, the quality of life in the 3rd team went down. We found ourselves playing against stronger opposition and sides who were fired up by the prospect of wiping the smile off a club that perhaps had got a little above itself. Third-team games became relentlessly disappointing and morale dropped further. Over the season we lost a series of mismatches by large margins and frequently trudged off the pitch grumpy and depressed.

A friend of mine used to wear a badge that sported the motto 'If all else fails, lower your standards'. All of a sudden, this seemed very helpful advice. The only way to get back to enjoyable rugby, I figured, was to start playing against worse sides in a lower league. The gentlemen of the various Surrey Rugby committees couldn't be relied upon to organise well-matched lower league games, given the secretive and mysterious nature of their decision-making process. Their decisions about promotion and relegation appeared to be made on the basis of confused nods and winks over a few beers rather than anything to do with the previous season's results.

The 3rd XV was the lowliest regularly playing side at Warlingham. There were very occasional 4th-team fixtures but they struggled to organise a side more than two or three times a season. If I was to get regular rugby against sides closer to my level, I was either going to have to find a way to influence Surrey Rugby politics and drag the 3rd team back down into easier matches, or make the 4th team a little more reliable.

And so, with that in mind, I found myself at the club's Annual General Meeting on a weekday evening, trying to see if I could somehow sort out the administrative arrangements that were leading to my side getting marmalised every week.

Will Carling, former Six Nations-winning England captain, was once sacked for complaining that rugby in Britain was run by fifty-seven old farts. In fact, it is run by several more than that. Every clubhouse throughout the country has its own group of elderly codgers, each contributing their own particular fragrance to the administration of the game.

The Warlingham AGM had gathered somewhere in the region of fifty-seven of its very own old farts into the club hall and as I arrived they were working their way fastidiously through the minutes of the previous year's meeting. The acoustics of the room made it almost impossible to work out what anyone was saying but it didn't seem to be the sort of meeting where anyone was actually listening to what anyone else was saying anyway.

Rugby club organisation is something of an oxymoron. Given that to rise to the top of any local club, one needs to have been around the club and, more importantly, its bar for several liver-busting decades, it is a minor miracle that it exists at all. Numerous well-meaning individuals take on the responsibility for keeping the clubs ticking over only to find that their collective lack of brainpower due to several decades of hard drinking makes the task almost impossible.

Having said that, Warlingham was fortunate in having an efficient, well-organised, sober, intelligent and coherent administrator at the heart of its organisation. This may not have been unrelated to the fact that she was a woman, thus somewhat immune from the weaknesses and predilections that afflict most members of the rugby community. Sally, in a part-time role, managed to rattle through the paperwork associated with keeping the club on track, a task that would have utterly stumped most former players.

Behind the scenes there are other important unsung heroes that keep a rugby club ticking along. There is a groundsman, who patiently marks out lines on the pitch and charts the lakes, rivers and swamps that appear every winter once the rains begin to fall. There are random drunken older men who gather for lunches once in a while to relive their glory days on the field, compare medical ailments and write out large cheques to keep the club finances in order. There are parents who coach and manage the junior teams and thus provide a steady stream of seventeen-year-olds to run around the pitch whilst the rest of us catch our breath. There are Honorary Treasurers and Honorary Secretaries who keep records and mutter under their breath at committee meetings. There are caterers and cleaners, voluntary or perhaps paid, and bar staff paid in either cash or the occasional free bag of dry roasted.

Examples of all these characters were gathered at the Warlingham AGM and were presided over by a rotund, bearded chairman. As they chuntered through the agenda, there were just three other active current rugby players, looking as confused and bewildered as I felt. These were the three captains-in-waiting, due to be nominated to take up the posts of running the top three sides for the coming season.

Third-team fly half Dave Rundle was looking to take over as 3rd-team captain. Dave Rundle was quite a keen bean, a good player and well organised. With a tactical appreciation of the game, he looked like the sort who would kick the 3rds into shape and get them into a position to survive and occasionally succeed in their competitive league. He was not the sort to negotiate a strategic relegation and drop the 3rds into a pool where my limited talents would be of use.

The three captains had all been duly proposed and seconded and were elected to their positions without dissent. The Chair wished them a successful season and moved on to the next item of business. There had been no mention of the 4th team whatsoever, so it looked as though, without a captain, the 4ths would be quietly forgotten about.

I've never been one to resist the possibility of being elected to some sort of office, however lowly. I had spent a number of years trying to break into politics and had even had a run-out as Liberal Democrat parliamentary candidate, albeit in the 50th-safest Conservative seat in the country. I'd been a local councillor and a school governor and on umpteen committees of one sort or another in my time. I shuffled round the room and had a quiet word in the ear of the Honorary Secretary. Before anyone had a chance to object I had been appointed the captain of the Warlingham 4th XV.

This had been far too easy. I hadn't had to deliver a leaflet or canvass a single voter. By the simple act of turning up, I had been appointed. Not so much rising to the dizzy heights but slipping unnoticed into a lowly office. Never had acquiring power and responsibility been so easy, but none the less I now had a title; captain. Perhaps now work colleagues would take me seriously. Maybe my children would listen to me when they realised that I was now in charge of the 4th XV or, to give it its more formal title, the Extra As.

Rugby teams within a club often have very strange titles. Rather than being clearly numbered from 1st team to 2nds, 3rds, 4ths and so on, many clubs use a confusing combination of letters and numbers or added names like the Occasionals or the Warriors etc. This is either to defend the sensitive egos of players – playing for the As might sound better than being dropped to the 3rds – or to allow fixtures secretaries the freedom to organise matches without necessarily revealing the relative strength of the side that they are putting out. At my little public school, for example, the sides all had Latin names and so for a little while I may have played for a side referred to as Extra Quam, which sounds more like a name for a vegetarian meat substitute. Even now I can't quite remember which classical tags were given to which side in which year and I suspect that was the whole point.

So as 4th XV or Extra A captain, I was now responsible for finding fourteen other players and getting them onto a rugby pitch with me often enough to honour a season's worth of league fixtures. If I could manage to do that more than two or three times over the course of the year, I would be doing better than my predecessor. The incentive for me was that the 4th XV played at the very bottom of the Surrey reserve team league structure. It was the only league in the county from which you could never be relegated, no matter how badly you played. There was nowhere lower to go.

I now had to recruit a team. I was going to have to look far and wide to find people to fit into the fifteen different positions on the pitch and a few spares who could be shoved in anywhere as the need arose. It wasn't just a case of finding fifteen beefcakes. Muscle-bound hunks would already be playing at a higher level. I needed new people who didn't know they could play or, failing that, I needed to persuade some rugby has-beens or never-really-quite-had-beens out of retirement. Looking around the fringes of the club there were a few likely suspects waiting to be asked to play. I just had to fit them into the right slots.

Chapter 6

Friends, Romans, Commuters! Lend Me Your Cauliflower Ears

Rugby is more than just a game played by men with odd-shaped balls. It is a game played by very odd-shaped men. Huge men with strange accents and few teeth; small, thin boys with more hair gel than body fat; and old men largely held together with gaffer tape and neoprene. There is a job on a rugby pitch for almost everyone, and all the positions require a different set of physical attributes and inclinations. Beyond the general separation between forwards and backs there are further variations and cross-breeds of rugby player.

Having established myself as a hooker, I needed to identify some regular and reliable props. These are the characters on either side of the hooker, in the front row of the scrum, who are usually the butt of jokes about their lack of mental and physical agility. What they do have to do is absorb, in their neck, shoulders and lower back, the combined pressure of sixteen men forced together over the ball.

Over my first few seasons, I had come across some fine, stout gentlemen who looked after me in the centre of scrum after scrum, resisting the pressure of opposition packs and allowing me to practise my fancy footwork whilst retrieving the ball. Men like Trevor Hutchins, a delivery driver during the week and immovable force at the weekend.

Trevor is large. There's no getting away from it. Obese doesn't even quite cover it. He has his own postcode and is one of the very few delivery men visible from space. There are not many sports that would seek out his own particular combination of inertia and padding. However, from my point of view, he is always a welcome addition to any rugby side I might play in.

The great advantage of a Trevor, or indeed any massively overweight front-row player, is that they take an awful lot of shifting. The last thing you want in a scrum is to be going backwards as you try and get your heel over the ball. With Trevor in a scrum, you were not likely to be moving anywhere. At the very worst, the scrum might pivot around him.

The other advantage of a Trevor is that when, as occasionally happens, a scrum or a maul collapses, with a bit of luck Trevor will be there to provide a soft landing. Many are the times when I have avoided impact with the hard ground by landing on Trevor's vast belly. It's always tempting to stay there for a bit longer, like a toddler in a bouncy castle, until your mother tells you to get off and put your shoes back on.

Props seem to survive a little longer than players of other positions in club rugby, in spite of what you might imagine would be an injury-prone role. This may be due to the fact that, for props, most of the impact is at low speed and under relatively controlled conditions. Unlike backs who hurtle around the pitch at great pace and then snap in two whenever they trip over each other, props will tend to amble gently from one scrum to the next and have a little more natural padding to protect their bones.

There is often a degree of maturity to be found in the front row. The stout and solid specimen of manliness that is Bob Nunn, for example, has been another great source of inspiration and insulation in many a game. Like me, he took up rugby at a more mature stage in life, having seen his son enjoying the sport. A local council officer, he has, through rugby, travelled to more places and met more people than his municipal employment could ever have possibly generated. Generally a thoroughly mild-mannered individual, he can be a demon grappler on the pitch and reminds me of those Saturday afternoon wrestlers on the 1970s television of my childhood.

In the second row of the scrum, characters like Dave Halliwell and Phil Evans, who had looked after my nose-busting Purley John Fisher opponent so effectively before, would be my first choice but it was also going to be a good place to stick any overweight but strongish-looking new recruits I could manage to find lurking around the club.

Moving to the back row of the scrum, the stakes are raised a little. This is the prime real estate on the rugby field and is usually reserved for the few members of the team who actually know what they are doing. Only required to hang loosely off the back and sides of the scrum, the flankers and number 8 can escape quickly and either run around with the ball or go running after whoever has got it. Quite often the boys who play here can tackle. Sometimes they know the rules and how to break them without getting caught.

In the lower sides, the back row is where you would typically place your ringers, players who should really be playing in higher teams in higher leagues but for reasons of organisational incompetence, petty disputes over training methods, drinking games gone wrong or being caught chatting up the captain's girlfriend, find themselves on your touchline looking for a game. They can't make it into the competitive positions in the higher sides so they drop down a team or two in search of glory.

I suspected that these would also be the easiest positions to fill. It is the sort of place where everyone seems to want to play. Close to the action but still able to enjoy some daylight and fresh air once in a while, without having your face squashed inside the darker corners of the scrum. Forward play is often referred to as 'the dark arts'. This is a wonderful bit of spin on behalf of the forward fraternity, suggesting that there is something mysterious and supremely intelligent and skilful about the role; a secret world of techniques around the fringes of the law that only true initiates can be allowed to know. It is of course nothing of the sort. They are called the dark arts because no one has the faintest idea what they are doing, rolling around in the mud wondering where the ball might be. We are all collectively 'in the dark'.

Another reason why they are called the dark arts is because, as a forward, you spend much of the game with your eyes shut, in a massive pile of blubber, not daring to open them in case you see something unpleasant up close and personal. There are things that happen inadvertently in forward playing situations that you just can't talk about. Not because they are illegal or deeply technical and tactical, but because they are awkward, embarrassing and rather intimate. Arms, hands and faces end up in places that really they would rather not be and so the least said about it the better.

I felt confident about the forwards and what they needed to do. Recruiting and looking after them would be fine. The backs, however, would be more complicated, as they occupied an aspect of the game I rarely saw. I was always last to emerge from the scrum, by which point the backs would often have completed the move they had been playing.

Backs are typically thin, fast and more conventionally good-looking. On a good day they run around a lot and score tries. On a bad day they stand around getting cold whilst the forwards keep the ball and huddle around it to keep warm.

Backs start at number nine with a strange hybrid called the scrum half. This is a tiny chap with a big voice and some serious mental health issues. Ideally here you are looking for someone with a severe Napoleon complex so that he can bark orders at the forwards without fear. He is like those small yappy dogs that seem to think they are huge Alsatians.

It helps if the scrum half can pass the ball quickly and confidently. This is because he is the smallest person on the pitch and as a result everyone wants to try and tackle him. On the very rare occasions when I have tackled anyone it has usually been the opposition scrum half just because he has been close enough for me not to have to run too far, small enough for me to get my arms round and usually stationary and looking in the opposite direction.

Scrum halves are normally very keen to get hold of something called 'clean ball' from the forwards. This does not mean that one of the forwards carries a J-cloth, some Marigolds and a bowl of washing-up water in order to provide a mud-free offering to the number 9. Clean ball is when the ball is placed gently and tidily at the back of a ruck, maul or scrum and all the opposition forwards are either intricately entwined within the seething mass of flesh or else lying in a heap somewhere else wheezing quietly to themselves having been run into the ground by your team's impressive command of the field.

With a clean ball thus delivered, the scrum half can then position himself delicately over the ball, survey the position and distribution of his fellow backs and then deliver a swift well-directed pass into the loving hands of the fastest available one who will then run off and score a try.

Sadly, in real rugby as played in the lower sides, clean ball is as elusive as a bar of soap in the communal bath. More often than not, when the ball pops out from between some unsuspecting or possibly unconscious forwards, it does so at high speed in an entirely unpredictable direction. It is then swiftly followed by two or three huge opposition forwards, drooling and baying for blood. At this stage all the scrum half can do is fling the ball backwards as quickly as possible, vaguely in the direction of one of his teammates, and hope that this distracts the marauding opposition pack and that they leave him alone and batter his colleague instead.

However, I was fortunate that I could rely on at least one person to regularly volunteer for the ritual abuse involved in playing in this position: Tom Osbourne, one of the first new players I had actually recruited after getting chatting to him at a Liberal Democrat street stall during some local elections. Aside from both being political animals, we also shared the distinction of being not very good at rugby but none the less keen to have a go. In spite of all the evidence to the contrary, Tom decided that being scrum half was his natural position, and in the absence of anyone else willing to take on the role, Tom regularly got the 4th-team number 9 shirt – much to the dismay of whoever ended up at number 10.

Number 10, the fly half, is the star role, the Jonny Wilkinson position. Here, a safe distance away from the forwards, I needed to identify a devilishly handsome, floppy-haired boy who would cope with whatever Tom threw at him and then decide what to do with it. I needed someone who could look after the rest of the backs and could kick the ball for restarts and through the posts once in a while.

I had occasionally played with one fly half who was a treat to play with: Dave, related to Big Tony of 'Peckham Rolex' and 'rugby ball up the jumper' fame. He had a wonderfully unconventional approach to the position and would always keep opposition backs and referees on their toes. He had one trick up his sleeve, which was always entertaining to watch. When in possession of the ball and faced with an opponent he couldn't run round and with no teammates he could rely on to catch a pass, he would bounce the ball off his own head, over his opponent, and then catch it and run on. This particular move would normally confuse the opposition and have the referee reaching for his rule book.

Dave did not have the floppy-haired, public schoolboy look often found in this position. His haircut was the sort normally classified in clipper settings. Sadly he was not the most reliable of players and you could never be really sure he would turn up for a game until he was on the pitch. I was going to have to keep my eye open for someone else to slot into the glamour role.

Beyond the fly half are found two backs referred to as the centres. This is because they spend most of the time standing around in the centre of the pitch, waiting for the ball. Ideally it will arrive in their hands in the form of a well-timed pass from the fly half. More often than not it will arrive firmly clutched to the chest of an opposition player and be accompanied by an outstretched hand, or possibly a fist.

Beyond the centres is the saddest, loneliest position on the rugby field – the wing. Here is where you place the smallest, thinnest players you have available in the hope that the least harm will come to them. Their job is to stand at the end of the long line of backs and wait for the ball. This can be a long wait, perhaps lasting several seasons. Many will die of hypothermia long before ever receiving a pass.

For a winger to get the ball, almost every single other member of the team needs to have done something right and they all need to have done it consecutively. This happens almost as rarely as winning the lottery, so poor wingers need to wrap up their delicate frame in layers of Lycra, goose fat and fleece and hope that the referee's final whistle blows before their fingers and toes snap off.

The wing is often home to the youngest players on the pitch, people like Chris Lock: a teenage stick insect who found himself lurking around the rugby club one Sunday afternoon watching a younger relative play in the junior section. Rugby clubs are dangerous places to lurk if you are an able-bodied male, even if, like Chris, you have all the physical attributes of a standard lamp. There is always the risk that you will be introduced to a persuasive captain on the hunt for extra players. Chris failed to run away quickly enough and as a result would be playing with me in the 4ths for several seasons.

The last position on the pitch, number 15, is the full back. This is the last man in the line of defence, who gets to make one final, usually futile, attempt at preventing an opposition try. He might occasionally join in the line of attack, but only if he is feeling particularly enthusiastic. Once in a while he will have to stand underneath a loftily kicked ball and attempt to catch it, whilst everyone is watching. This can be tricky as he may need to find somewhere to stub out his cigarette first.

Full back is normally the home of the more experienced player, who would like to be on the pitch mostly so he can get a better view of the game, rather than exert himself in any particular way. It is a good spot from which to make helpful suggestions to one's teammates, the opposition or the referee, whilst everyone else is trying to catch their breath.

A fairly casual approach to rugby and life in general is usually found at full back. One of my all-time favourite full backs, Robin Ellingham, once turned up for a game when we were particularly desperate for players, having just said to his wife that he was popping out to get some potatoes. He played for us, made a couple of tackles and had a little run with the ball and then returned home to finish cooking the dinner.

Mark Bright was another great full back; not because he was particularly good at tackling, kicking, passing or any of that stuff, just because he will always make up a side, play in absolutely any position and stay for a pint or two afterwards. An award-winning TV editor by day, he spends his working week in a darkened Soho edit suite, where hot and cold production runners tend to his every need. At the weekend it's as much as he can do to pull his boots on and amble onto the pitch. If he can find time for a pint before the game, all the better.

So there were a few players I could identify to make up the 4ths but there were also a few gaps. Every week it began to be a mammoth struggle to find fourteen other people to fill all these positions and get a side out.

Chapter 7

Struggling in Streatham

Worrying about getting a side together for each game took over virtually my entire life. I attended training sessions at the club, not with the view of getting any exercise, but with the sole intention of identifying players who might be available at the weekend and had been overlooked by the other coaches. I was on hand in case a new potential player turned up and could come and have a tryout with the 4ths before one of the other captains snapped him up.

At every social event I went to, I was on the lookout for men of any shape or size who could be persuaded to come and play. Old friends were contacted solely for the purpose of seeing if they could be persuaded to turn out and help me make up the numbers. Work colleagues were cajoled into joining me at the weekend for a game. It was all I could do to restrain myself from approaching complete strangers on the train on the way to work, if they looked like they could handle themselves on a rugby pitch. One way or another I had to get fifteen names onto a team sheet so that we could fulfil our first 4th-XV league fixture away against Streatham Croydon at the beginning of September, which was just a week away.

The first place to start putting together a side was at the club selection meeting on Tuesday evening. This was a gathering of all the club captains and the coach around a noticeboard in a corner of the committee room. On the board was a selection of pegs set out in rows and the names of players on little plastic tags. Players who had declared their availability were then allocated to the various positions in the various teams and when the first three sides had filled all their pegs, I was left with the scraps.

Several frantic phone calls and text messages later and luckily I had fifteen names. Included in my first side was Seb Slater, a new recruit at work who had recently graduated from Goldsmiths College where he had played rugby fairly regularly. He brought along a mate and offered himself up as full back. Also in the side was my mate Jim Tandy who had never played rugby in his life but is tough and strong as he spends his weeks shifting heavy loads as a gardener and builder. As a new player he was of course destined for the second row, filling the last and least popular position on the pitch. Messages and directions were sent out and on Saturday afternoon we gradually assembled at the opposition's ground for our first fixture of the season.

Streatham Croydon's ground is situated, as you might imagine, roughly halfway between Streatham and Croydon, somewhere in Thornton Heath, tucked away behind Mayday Hospital, just off the A23. It is an old club with a proud history, a large concrete stand and cold concrete changing rooms underneath. The showers are somewhat more Dartmoor Prison than Dolphin bathrooms but they have two decent pitches surrounded by a high chain-link fence. It is an ethnically diverse area and the lower side was captained by a large, round and moustachioed Muslim called Abdul. I had played against him a couple of times for the 3rds, but this was my first encounter with him as captain of the 4ths.

Streatham Croydon also had another shorter and rounder Middle Eastern-looking player with a little goatee beard, who seemed to be known as Arnie. He looked like a forward, short and thickset, but for some reason he lined up with the backs as the game kicked off. Only once he got the ball did we realise why. It was as though Usain Bolt had put on a fat suit. He powered through our hastily cobbled together defences like a steam train to score a succession of easy tries. Recriminations were flying around between my players and my first game as captain looked set to become an embarrassing humiliation.

My little brother Nathan was one of the few members of our team making any real impact on the game. He was tackling hard but being tackled even harder. The Streatham players set about trying to slow him down and singled him out for particular attention. They were keen to put in their tackles on him with just a little more aggression than might otherwise be necessary. Naturally I got all big-brotherly and defensive in response, dragging myself over to where he was being held down as fast as I could and ferociously trying to get their players off him. There was nothing like a bit of fraternal bonding to fire up my game, although I'm not sure how helpful it was for Nathan to have his wheezing, overweight, elderly relative collapsing on top of the pile of players around him as he was trying to extract himself.

The other great thing about playing with Nathan was that every now and again he would pick up the ball from the back of a ruck and run off with it. If I was lucky and in the right place at the right time, I could tag along for the ride. A couple of times, I managed to grab hold of a bit of his shirt and together we would crash through the opposition forwards knocking them out of our way as we went. Nathan provided the strength and sense of direction and determination. I provided some extra weight and padding. It seemed to be a good arrangement.

At half-time, however, the opposition had lots of points and we had none. I was exhausted and had no ideas about how we could improve our game. All I had to fall back on was some vaguely remembered management coaching advice about constructive feedback, the principle behind which being that you wrap some genuine praise for some aspect of the job done well around a constructive suggestion of something people could choose to do differently. Like a hamburger, you give the meat of the message wrapped in something soft and fluffy like a sesame seed bun.

To be honest we hadn't done a huge amount worthy of praise other than turning up, but there had been some great tackles from Seb and others. Without them, of course, we would have been even further behind. My strategic understanding of the game being minimal, the only change I could suggest was that we stop moaning and complaining at each other when someone made a mistake, which was quite often. Although I could barely breathe after an exhausting forty minutes, something of these thoughts was incorporated into my half-time team talk.

As we huddled together passing around water bottles and orange segments, I raved with as much passion as I could muster about Seb's heroic try-saving stops and every single other positive moment I could remember from the first half. As I began to ramble, I realised I hadn't the faintest idea why we were losing, other than they must have been just better than us, so sadly I had nothing tactical or strategic to offer by way of advice. At that point I gave up and handed over the floor to someone, anyone, who had half an idea of something we could try and do differently. Meanwhile, I caught my breath and girded my loins for a final peroration about how no one, but no one, was allowed to waste any of their breath criticising teammates on the pitch.

Over the rest of the season this last bit of my first team talk would evolve into the 4th-team motto, that 'no one gives anyone any sh*t for being sh*t'. I took the view that we were all playing for fun, for pleasure, and that in my side many were playing as a personal favour to me. The last thing I wanted was to be part of a team where anyone was attacked or humiliated for being a bit rubbish. We were all a bit rubbish, but at least we were there playing a game of rugby rather than lying at home asleep on the sofa in front of *Channel 4 Racing*. I wanted these boys to come back and play for me again week after week and they weren't going to if the whole game consisted of other players telling them how hopeless they were.

We lined up again to face the Streatham onslaught. The team talk seemed to have some sort of an effect and early in the second half we won a penalty near the opposition try line. Rather than opting to take some points by kicking for goal, we opted for a quick tap and run move. Sadly we didn't quite manage to break through the Streatham defences, but we had at least made our presence felt on the pitch.

Not long later we gave away a scrum in our own half. With the opposition putting the ball in, our chances of getting the ball were limited. However, with my mate Jim pushing behind me in the scrum I somehow managed to win the ball, and by the time I emerged from the scrum, one of our backs was sprinting over their try line and touching the ball down. Finally we had some points on the board and with a conversion, we had two more.

Streatham may have had 68 points but at least we had 7 to our name. It wasn't much, but as the final whistle blew we made our way back to the changing rooms with a little pride still intact. We had survived. The 4ths were in business and, as we enjoyed the post-match tray of roast potatoes in the Streatham and Croydon bar, we chatted and made plans for the rest of the season. I was going to need to rustle up some more players and we were all going to need to play a little better somehow. Still, we were on our way and it looked like it could be fun.

Chapter 8

Igor the Terrible

In his seminal work, *Bowling Alone*, Robert Putnam talks about the collapse in membership of societies and clubs in America since the 1950s. During the post-war era, thousands of Americans were members of bowling clubs and would compete in leagues and build friendships and networks of contacts. In Putnam's view these contributed to something called social capital, which created strong, healthy and safe communities. Nowadays most Americans, if they still take part in the sport, will bowl alone.

Although I was quite pleased with myself for getting the 4th XV going again, older members of Warlingham rugby club were not particularly impressed. They would recall wistfully the days long gone when the club would turn out a 5th, 6th or even a 7th side. There were apparently, once upon a time, regular, annual club tours to exotic locations all over the world and a packed programme of well-attended social events in and around the club. Sadly, now it seemed to be harder and harder every year to keep sides and social events going. Volunteers to do all the little jobs needed to keep the club ticking over seem to be difficult to find and persuading people to do important things on committees proved to be almost impossible.

Putnam, after extensive statistical analysis, found that the strongest factor linked to the decline in club and society membership was the rise in the number of hours spent watching the television. As Americans spent more and more time in front of the goggle-box, they spent less and less time meeting and interacting with their neighbours and doing things together. Watching sport on TV has over the years squeezed out participating in sports in local clubs. The more money and time we invest in our domestic TV-viewing experience, the less we spend on our real-world experiences.

Rugby is not a sport you can play on your own. It needs other players but also other people to sort out fixtures, put out flags and post protectors. It needs referees and it needs people to type all the scores into a computer so that the leagues make some sort of sense. There are forms to fill out, registrations to complete and local authorities to be apprised and appeased. Little wonder that, for many, the prospect of relaxing on the sofa with a beer and a tube of Pringles for a high definition, surround sound, audio-visual experience is much more enticing than helping out in a grubby local rugby club.

In the modern world it seems far more socially acceptable to burn off the calories in a world of your own, iPod strapped to your upper arm and headphones blocking your ears as you pound away on a treadmill in an expensive gym. In these soulless temples to body fascism, woe betide anyone who tries to start a conversation or offer to buy a round of drinks. Just keep your eyes fixed on one of the many 42-inch flat screen TVs positioned on the walls around the equipment, as the LED display tells you how far you would have run if you had been outdoors, and how many calories you have burned off.

In building up a new 4th team I did feel like I was swimming against the tide. There was often a sense of resignation about the poor prospects of getting a side together for any game. Club members would often think that it was better to merge or amalgamate teams rather than run the risk of two sides being under-resourced. Worn down by the effort of holding a club together and the lack of people willing to put themselves out to get involved, club officials are never really sure what to do with someone new who wants to make a go of a new initiative.

Judging by their bewildered looks, work colleagues probably thought I was mad to be playing a team sport at all, let alone one that involved such extreme violence and intimate physical contact with other men. As for captaining a side, wasn't that faintly ridiculous for a short, overweight middle-aged man, to have ideas so clearly above his station? The only acceptable sporting outlet for gentlemen of my age appears to be an annual long-distance individual endurance challenge like a marathon or a cross-continent cycle ride for 'charidee'. I could raise money to strengthen community spirit, that's acceptable, but participating in a sport that involved other people and actually creating some kind of community spirit – that's just weird.

Fortunately there were just about enough people who seemed to need to do something other than go shopping and watch *The X Factor* on a Saturday; like-minded souls who seemed to have a need to interact with real people in real life rather than botox- and silicone-enhanced pretend people in celebrity land. I found them propping up the bar in the rugby club. People like John Glover and his family. My search for players for the 4th XV seemed to resonate with the Glover family.

John is head of a little rugby-playing dynasty and is one of the reasons I still can't retire from rugby. He is hovering somewhere in his fifties having played continuously at Warlingham for several decades. He may have all his own hair but it is very grey. He is the original silver scrummager. As long as he still makes himself available for selection, I find it very difficult to contemplate retiring, no matter how old and infirm I'm feeling.

One of the reasons John seems to keep playing is that he has an almost Munchausian obsession with other people's injuries. As soon as someone on either side begins to experience a slight twinge, John is there like a shot, dispensing medical attention and advice. As a result he became known affectionately as Doctor Glover in spite of having no formal medical training whatsoever. He took his role seriously and even began stepping out with a nurse, who would occasionally be seen on the touchline and on hand to offer slightly more professionally qualified first aid as required.

John was always among the first to respond to my requests for players and as a result got his name first onto the team sheet. He became a regular and reliable member of the 4ths and, despite his advancing years, would provide a welcome injection of aggression into the forward contests with a good strong shove in the scrum.

John also has a couple of rugby-playing sons and both came in rather handy for our next home fixture against another local rival side, Croydon Shirley Wanderers. His son Alex was 1st-team captain so didn't play for us, but he did send a few of his old rugby-playing school friends in my direction: a bunch of city boys living in Clapham with plenty of banter but also a reasonable level of skill. John's other son Christopher did come along to play with us and turned out to be quite a handy all-purpose back. Even more importantly he brought with him a tiny little friend called Igor. Half-Russian, half-pixie and with a shaggy mop of hair, Igor lined up on the wing as we kicked off for this local derby game.

With Dr Glover and another senior player, 1970s wrestler lookalike Bob Nunn, in the forwards we had quite a lot of fun and managed to bundle the ball through the Croydon pack. At one point Glovers senior and junior linked up as Christopher popped up a little pass to his dad and sent him over the try line to collect five points.

The Clapham boys all played well, although their city lunches and corporately entertained lifestyles had possibly taken a little toll on their fitness. Igor, however, was extraordinary. Despite his tiny frame he was tackling and stopping players twice his size and with his mop of hair flopping all over the place he spent the afternoon running rings round the opposition whenever we could get the ball to him. He gained the title Igor the Terrible and cult status in subsequent match reports.

With or without the ball Igor was a force to be reckoned with. If he spotted an opposition player within range he would dart towards him. Something about the way he moved would disorientate attackers more used to the slow steady approach of a lumbering centre. With his arms, legs, hips and hair all moving independently in opposite directions, Igor would startle and bewilder anyone from the other team who got the ball. He didn't always need to tackle them. Sometimes opposition players would just fall over as a result of looking at him. It was as if he had a team of KGB agents hidden in the nearby bushes, firing miniature darts filled with uranium and horse tranquillisers at the backs of their legs.

Although my side was comfortably in the lead, I found myself struggling slightly to keep up with the pace. This turned out to be quite a good thing. I was having a little rest and catching my breath some distance away from the centre of the action, when gradually the play moved towards me. I was playing the role of the mountain, as the old saying goes, and the ball was playing the part of Mohammed. By the time the game got to where I was, I had more or less recovered and by chance seemed to be in the right place at the right time, just behind a little pile of players.

One of the Clapham boys, John Burrell, was playing at scrum half and extracted the ball from out of the heap of arms and legs on the ground in front of me. As he looked up the first thing in his field of vision turned out to be me. More experienced Warlingham players would have known at that point to look around for someone else, who might actually be able to catch the ball. My remedial handling skills were well known throughout the club. However, young Mr Burrell, with impeccable manners, delivered one of the most gentle and beautifully timed passes to his new captain and suddenly I found myself with an uninterrupted view of the try line. A short sprint later I was over the line, collapsing onto the ground with the ball tucked under my arm and a massive grin on my face.

A combination of a strategic breather and a little deference from a well-brought-up corporate banker and I had my first ever, proper try. This was no charity try. The scrum half had reasonably expected the team captain would be able to catch a ball and score a try and, as it turned out on this occasion, I could. It wasn't just that I had been in the right place at the right time, but we had the right team against the right opposition on the right pitch, at home against local rivals. The Warlingham 4th team seemed like the place to be.

Sadly we couldn't hold onto Igor for very long. After a couple of games with us he was, we assumed, whisked away by his minders and smuggled back to Mother Russia in a diplomatic bag.

Chapter 9

Never Work with Children (or Committees)

When politicians and policy wonks think about participation in sport they are not thinking about themselves or their generation. They are thinking about children. Young people apparently need to be bullied, bribed, cajoled or coerced to shape up, get active and take part in some wholesome calorie-burning activity, in the name of a crusade against childhood obesity. Ideally they should do that under the supervision of a suitably qualified, fully insured and CRB-checked professional, so that their parents can get on with Internet shopping, growing a middle-aged spread and watching Jeremy Kyle on the TV.

Sport for young people has changed in my lifetime from something you did a bit at school and, with jumpers for goalposts, you did a bit at the weekend in the local park. At Devonshire Primary in Sutton back in the 1970s it was so rare for anyone to take part in organised sport outside school that if they did the Headmaster would organise a special assembly about them. One boy out of a school of several hundred played for a little-league football team and stood at the front of the hall showing us his prized medal for winning his league. We were in awe, but he made it very clear that his club was definitely not looking for more players, so we were not to go and get any funny ideas about joining in. Elspeth Moore was a member of a swimming club and won the occasional gala and that was it.

Nowadays, throughout suburbia, parks and playing fields are packed with parents standing on touchlines shouting at their offspring to run, tackle, shoot and score. Medals, trophies and certificates are awarded by the crate-load every week. Thousands and thousands of young boys are dragged out of bed on Saturday and Sunday mornings by parents keen to produce the next David Beckham or Jonny Wilkinson. Their tiny offspring are kitted out in expensive boots and replica shirts and forced to live out their parents' failed dreams. The mums and dads, however, very rarely seem to get involved in anything more energetic than a brisk walk to the clubhouse to grab a bacon buttie.

Whilst I was playing rugby myself, of course I wasn't immune to the desire to give my own offspring the opportunity to get involved in the game. I too wanted my son Dexter to become the talented and successful rugby player I had no hope of becoming myself. So, although I had barely recovered from playing on a Saturday, every Sunday morning I would drag my aching body and my bellyaching boy child out of bed and back to the club.

Countless hours are spent driving little darlings to and from muddy playing fields. Hundreds of pounds are spent on making sure they have the regulation kit and safety equipment. All across the country coaches spend days on courses collecting certificates and studying manuals and are the little darlings grateful? Are they hell! My own poor child was small in his age group due to the combination of my genes and a birthday late in the school year. He couldn't quite fathom why his parent who supposedly loved him would inflict so much pain, cold and discomfort on him throughout his childhood. He would whine about the weather, whinge about the wet and moan about the mud. Still I made him play. I was determined he would learn the skills that I lacked. My frustrations at not being able to play the game properly were directed into forcing this poor little child into a game that really wasn't for him.

I would help out with the coaching most Sundays, borrowing exercises from training with the senior players and introducing them to the boys in the mini and junior sections. Running through the stretches with them was also a good way to get my body moving again after the exertions of the game on Saturday and a good way to clear the head after the excesses of the previous evening. Dexter, however, would clown about and do his best to avoid getting hurt or do anything that felt too much like exercise.

Dexter may have hated it but I really enjoyed running around with the boys on a Sunday morning. I would hold tackle pads for them to crash into and have them running through drills that the 1st team used. I gained some credibility by virtue of the fact that I played at a senior level although when I reported back on the sometimes rather dismal 4th-team scorelines they were less than impressed. I tended to be drawn towards the second string in our squad of younger players, rather than the ones who from an early age were showing signs of taking the game and themselves far too seriously. I liked the kids who, clumsy and utterly gormless, struggled as I had done to do the simple things like catching the ball, running in a straight line and passing. Over a few seasons I was able to watch them mature a little, gain some sort of command over their own limbs and acquire from somewhere their own full set of gorms.

Sadly, watching some of the better players in the squad reminded me of all the reasons I had hated sport as a child. Several of the kids who were naturally very good at the game, had such a single-minded determination to play well and win that they seemed to forget how to be pleasant human beings. In a few, a nasty prima-donna tendency would emerge. The odd pushy parent would attempt to throw their weight around trying to secure a more prominent role for their child prodigy. There were tears and tantrums although, to be fair, those were mostly from the coaches.

The game is so much better to take part in as a grown-up rather than as a child. Young boys can be extremely cruel and unkind to each other. When one drops a catch or misses a tackle the rest are merciless in their reaction. If they can put each other down they will. As a coach I couldn't use my 4th-team motto about no one giving anyone any sh*t for being sh*t without offending their delicate little ears, and my attempts to instil the philosophy behind it using milder language rather failed. It's hardly surprising that team sports are so unpopular when they are mostly played by people before they have developed the social skills needed to enjoy the game to the full. Perhaps if more parents played, their children might see the depth of enjoyment that can be obtained from the game, whether as an individual you are any good at it or not.

The main reason why it is a struggle to keep young people playing sport is laundry. The very patient, tolerant and understanding Mrs Gauge would struggle during the winter months to clean three bags full of muddy kit that we managed between us to generate over a weekend. There were times when she needed to have a large glass of rosé before feeling brave enough to unzip the holdalls and tip out the filthy, wet and stinking contents and transfer them into the washing machine. This was, I'm told, particularly bad if the bag had been fermenting in the car boot for a few days before I remembered to bring it in. Once or twice it might have been simpler and more profitable to hand the bags over to a garden centre for them to sell on as garden compost.

Gradually the other boys got bigger and Dexter didn't. Wild height discrepancies caused by the random onset of adolescence throughout the team and their opponents meant that it no longer felt or looked very safe on the under-13s' pitches. It was fine for Dexter, but I was terrified. Whenever it was time for some tackling practice and I needed to hold up the foam pads for them to run at, I was at serious risk of being knocked over. Great steaming grumpy teenagers would compete to see which one of them could flatten me during the drills and exercises.

Rather than risk life and limb continuing as a coach to the under 13s, I tried my hand at refereeing. Mini and junior rugby teams are very rarely blessed with proper, trained referees. Parents or coaches are normally drafted in but each has their very different understanding of the rules. This is not helped by the fact that the regulations change as you go from one school year to the next. The rules are also periodically altered in response to a concern about the health and safety of the children playing. Keeping up to date as a referee requires a level of research, attention to detail and feats of memory more akin to autistic trainspotters and VAT inspectors. No surprise then that referees turn out to be an odd bunch.

In the younger age groups, no one is normally too bothered about going to the trouble of organising a neutral referee. The home side will rustle up a parent or coach to wield the whistle and everyone typically lets them get on with it. They might be biased, they might miss things, but the game is more important than the result. The atmosphere on the touchline is generally fairly relaxed and you don't tend to see the screaming, shouting and occasional acts of random violence associated with football. For most parents, it is important that their child gets to run around a bit, burn off some energy and make some friends. If they can pal up with the child whose parents have a huge people carrier then with a bit of luck they can transport your offspring to away matches and you can stay in bed with the Sunday papers. There are not that many pushy parents on rugby touchlines. There are more parents who at a push will stay outside in the wind and cold for about five minutes before retreating to the clubhouse for a coffee and a bacon roll.

Some clubs do get a little more touchy about the refereeing and invoke a little-used clause in the RFU children's rugby handbook that allows for two referees, one from each club, to oversee the two separate halves of the game, the theory being that neither side can then complain that the referee is biased. The two referees should balance each other out and ensure a fair and equitable outcome. This is of course complete nonsense as I discovered as we took our team to a nearby local rival one Sunday morning.

Under 13s are a fickle bunch. The team we were playing had picked up a few former Warlingham players and so there was a little bit of an edge to this particular fixture. Their coach had ever so slightly got under the collective skins of my coaching colleagues in previous seasons by being just a little bit too aggressive and shouty and too bothered about the result. The kids were nice enough but we hadn't taken terribly well to the chap who was looking after them.

As the boys warmed up with their usual routine of jumping onto the tackle pads, jumping on each other and throwing rugby balls at each other's heads, the coaches shook hands and sorted out the arrangements. The air of awkward animosity between the two sides meant that the two-referee option was suggested and agreed. I was given the honour of overseeing the second half and had a rummage around in my kitbag for a whistle, notepad and HB pencil. Jogging up and down the touchline during the first half I got the distinct impression that their referee was singling out our players for punishment and offering a very harsh interpretation of the rules to our boys, whilst his own seemed to be incapable of causing an infringement. It was as though he was getting his retaliation in first. He seemed to have decided that I was inevitably going to favour my own players and so he needed to do the same whilst he had the chance. At the end of the first half we were miles behind and my players were looking decidedly grumpy.

Now I'd like to think that I rose above this pre-emptive refereeing strike as I took charge for the second half. I would have hoped that I would have ignored my opposite number's blatant cheating and been scrupulously and unflinchingly fair. Sadly of course I wasn't. It wasn't that I was deliberately trying to redress the balance and fix the game in favour of my son and his mates. It's just that I was so enraged by the decisions in the first half that my senses were heightened to any transgression by the other team. There was a hair trigger in my mind, as I watched every little move of theirs like a hawk. My reaction time from offence to whistle was in nanoseconds. If my own side did anything questionable there was always a moment of doubt and my team got the benefit of it.

Normally, when I had previously refereed whole games, I would go out of my way to be stricter to my own side, partly to demonstrate my impartiality and partly to make sure my team learnt the rules and played within them. Most other referees I had seen were the same; tough on their own kids and forgiving to their guests. The split-duty refereeing seems to bring out the worst in everyone.

At the end of the game, which, strangely enough, we won, I went to shake hands with my fellow referee from the first half.

'I'm not going to tell you what I thought of that performance,' he said, and then proceeded to tell me anyway. It was apparently the worst refereeing display he had seen in all his life and, having read their diaries, the lives of his father, grandfather and great grandfather. He had in fact consulted with a rugby archivist in a dusty basement in Twickenham by phone during the match and my grasp of the rules had apparently been weaker and more feeble than anyone ever in the history of the game. He pointed towards sobbing children who had been deprived of their rightful and deserved victory by my cruel and contemptible display. I should be ashamed of myself and ideally go away and die. I exaggerate a little, but that was the general gist. The words 'pot', 'kettle' and 'black' came to mind but I bit my tongue. He was a lot bigger than me, had several larger mates and a pack of angry teenagers baying for my blood. I wanted to get out alive. I declined a post-match beer, went home and threw away the whistle.

Blaming my son's dwindling interest in the game I withdrew from involvement in the junior game for my own safety and concentrated on the happier, gentler and altogether more civilised version to be had with the adult 4th team. Dexter headed off to the slightly less hazardous pursuits of skateboarding, trampolining and mountain biking and I stuck to grappling with the Sunday papers, risking nothing more dangerous than a paper cut or a mild harrumphing over a provocative columnist's reactionary views.

I did, however, find my way onto the hallowed body known as The Committee, the governing body of the club that ran things, as an alternative way to fill up my time. Sports clubs all need some sort of constitutional body to take decisions and set the direction for the organisation. Fine, upstanding citizens, not content with merely spending their weekends in or around the rugby club, opt to spend a few extra weekday evenings there as well, reading over minutes, financial reports and membership numbers. It's a thankless but necessary task and one that I was invited to join.

It is said that a camel is a horse designed by committee and after sitting on a few (committees that is, not camels) I can understand why. There is something odd that happens to people once they are raised to the exalted status of committee member. Otherwise affable and agreeable individuals are transformed into irritable, obstructive and petulant pedants. It happens to the nicest people and has no doubt happened to me. I have seen it in local government and on school governor boards and in parent–teacher associations. Rugby clubs are no different. Take a seasoned drinker, always happy to buy a round in the bar, or a wonderful and resourceful mum, put them in a room together with an agenda and a collection of other fine worthy individuals and before long they will be squabbling and sulking like three-year-olds. Players and former players, whose barroom banter is second to none, become tongue-tied and diffident the minute the chairman brings the meeting to order.

I think perhaps the problem with committees is that they are magnets for the congenitally grumpy. The sort of people who are bothered and unhappy with the way a club is run will sometimes find their way onto the committee in order to 'Sort Things Out'. It turns out then that they are just bothered and unhappy with life generally and switch the focus of their disgruntlement towards fellow members of the committee. Anyone generally content and happy with life will drift along without ever opting to read through a treasurer's report or refer back to point 3.2 on the agenda.

I was invited to join the committee, not because I was unhappy with anything about the club but, I thought, because I was doing a reasonable job running the 4th team. It was probably more to do with an internal committee power struggle over some unfathomable feud. I sat through meeting after meeting wondering what on earth I was doing there and whose side I was supposed to be on. Meanwhile a group of people, who were supposed to be doing this for fun, squabbled and bickered like eight-year-olds in the back of a Ford Cortina on a hot sticky journey to Weston-super-Mare.

'And now,' said the chairman after the minutes had been agreed and the treasurer's and 1st-team manager's reports had been received, 'I would like to move onto the matter of Membership Subscriptions.'

Extracting money out of rugby players for the purpose of anything other than buying alcohol is like getting blood from a stone that has been baked in a thermonuclear reactor for three or four decades, just on the off chance that there might have been a small bloodsucking insect fossilised inside it. Rugby clubs struggle every year to make ends meet and collecting a few quid off the members every so often is an important part of keeping the club afloat. The subscriptions pay for things like heating and lighting the clubhouse, washing the shirts and feeding hungry players after every game. Some clubs collect match fees from every player as well as a membership sub from players, supporters and drinkers alike. The problem is that the captains and coaches of the different sides just want players, from wherever they can find them and of the best possible quality. Many a captain will turn a blind eye to the star player who has once again forgotten to bring his standing order form or any cash, but has just scored three or four tries.

Committee members would regularly get seriously aerated about this or that player who was apparently freeloading on the rest of the membership by failing to put his hand in his pocket and contribute to the costs of running the club. A handful of the better 1st-team players, perhaps harbouring fantasies of playing professionally somewhere, would mutter quietly that they put their bodies on the line for the club week after week, providing entertainment and results, and surely that was enough. Draconian sanctions were regularly discussed at committee meetings to name, shame and even drop non-paying players. Coaches and captains would pretend not to hear the new rules and select the non-paying players anyway, as they struggled to get sides together to honour the fixtures. Meanwhile, casual players would amble along postponing the point when they had to part with any cash for as long as possible and carefully avoiding the membership secretary in the bar.

Any business run like this would of course go bust within weeks. Somehow, however, rugby clubs seem to survive, without ever fully resolving this problem. Eventually people seem to have a rummage down the back of the sofa and stump up their membership subscription. Most will also put a fair amount of cash behind the bar, doing their bit by selflessly sacrificing their liver for the financial well-being of the club. Well-organised clubs find sponsors and patrons who, in exchange for an advertising hoarding around the pitch or a mention in the match programme, cough up enough money to keep the accountant from having a coronary.

The other trick up the rugby club treasurer's sleeve is the allocation of international match tickets. A large chunk of the tickets for England's fixtures at Twickenham is allocated to local clubs who then dish them out by ballot. You have to be a fully paid-up member to qualify for the ballot and so your membership subscription will need to be up to date. Ageing gentlemen who wouldn't dream of pulling on a pair of boots will remain members for many years in order to be in with a chance of securing tickets for the Six Nations tournament fixtures in the faint hope that Erica Roe will return one day for a second showing of her ample assets.

I stayed on the committee for as long as I could bear, trying to inject a friendly dose of good humour and reasonableness as best I could into the lengthy and tedious debates. Eventually, though, I came to the conclusion that it was more entertaining and instructive to listen to my own children fighting over the TV remote control than to spend one more minute listening to grown men and women arguing about missing standing orders or administrative edicts from the RFU. Somehow the club has survived and continues to survive without my guiding influence and in spite of the rows and wrangles that no doubt rumble on.

Chapter 10

International Duty

As I somehow managed to get a 4th side out regularly enough to honour our league fixtures, my standing within Warlingham Rugby Club was on the rise. In contrast, my professional career was on a distinct plateau. I had taken over as the head of a small charity doing bits of inner-city regeneration, as part of a national federation. I had inherited a disgruntled team and had no idea where my predecessor had hidden the gruntles. Funding was tight and instead of finding more I was getting bogged down in endless strategic reviews and trustee squabbles.

I had never quite got the hang of corporate hierarchies. I might not be all that good at mapping out and implementing a corporate strategy and my staff management skills were somewhere south of David Brent. I couldn't motivate my staff at work for love nor money.

But on a Saturday afternoon I was a leader of men. I could persuade fifteen chaps of all ages to put their body on the line for nothing more than a pat on the back and a share of a post-match jug of beer. Not only that, but senior club figures in brightly coloured club blazers sought me out on a Saturday evening in the bar, shook my hand firmly and enquired about my team's progress. I might not be much of a corporate player but here in Warlingham, I was sending an additional thirty or so thirsty players into the clubhouse after every home fixture and doing my bit to boost the club's profit and loss account.

The confirmation that all was going remarkably well for me within the club came in the form of a tap on the shoulder from one of the senior blazer brigade and an invitation to join a rather exclusive tour to France.

Somewhere in the dim and distant past, a few players from lowly Warlingham forged a link with one of the top clubs in France, Stade Français. As a result, every year when England play France, a fixture is arranged between a side from Warlingham and a team made up of veterans and a sprinkling of younger amateurs from the Paris club called the Old Hirelings. The selection of the Warlingham side for this prestigious fixture is conducted on the basis of nods, winks and quite possibly the odd Masonic handshake. I was now being invited to join in.

The England–France international fixture, otherwise known as 'Le Crunch', was to be played in Paris this year and fortunately coincided with a weekend free of 4th-XV fixtures. One of my very occasional 4th-team players, Peter Braithwaite, had booked us seats on the Eurostar and another club member had organised rooms in a reasonably priced Paris hotel. It wasn't going to be a cheap weekend, however, and as I settled into my seat on the train I was surrounded by some of the wealthier Warlingham members. A tanned, moisturised and well-groomed chap pulled an expensive-looking bottle of champagne out of an expensive-looking leather weekend bag as we eased out of St Pancras.

'Care for a drop?' he asked.

'Don't mind if I do,' I replied.

Nigel, the champagne provider, was not someone I had seen around the club before. He turned out to be a delightfully genial property developer who had played regularly for the club a few years earlier before withdrawing to spend more time with his money. Every other year, however, he dug out his boots and made his way to Paris for this particular fixture. Nigel's champagne and a few other strategic beers kept us all well lubricated throughout the journey.

Elegant property developer aside, the rest of my travelling companions were a fairly ropey-looking bunch. There was I, heading off to apparently the most romantic city in Europe, with a motley collection of battered and bruised old forwards, with vast bellies, bright red noses and cauliflower ears. I would soon be wandering wistfully down the Champs-Élysées, accordion music playing somewhere in the background, and elegant Parisians looking on through a cloud of Gitanes smoke; arm in arm with the likes of people called Crackers and Smudger, both of whom could win a gurning competition without breaking sweat. Paris may be a city for lovers, but not this particular weekend.

As the rooms were allocated at our reasonably priced hotel, I found myself sharing with the delightful Graham Field. Fieldy is one of my favourite props and had played at 1st-team level but had no objection to joining in the odd game in the lowly 4ths with me. He confessed over a beer that he had been playing the game for twenty-eight years and had never yet learnt the rules. His view is that in each game and for each referee, the best players are those who play just on the limit of what they can get away with. Whatever the rule book might say that year, how any individual game is played is down to what the man with the whistle knows, sees and can be bothered to enforce.

Much of the game is effectively self-regulated. This is nowhere more true than in the front row. Here in the middle of the scrum it is next to impossible for a referee to see what is really going on. So the responsibility for maintaining some semblance of order falls to experienced props like Mr Field.

Graham told me a story of a player he used to come up against, who had a bit of a reputation for biting. Now this is not pleasant and is generally frowned upon. The last thing you want in the middle of a scrum, when you are worrying about keeping your neck and back in one piece, is to have some ugly, stubbly prop gnawing at your earlobes. I've no idea why some people think it is a good idea and fortunately it is very rare.

When Graham found himself being nibbled in one of the early forward encounters of a game, he decided to 'go down' – lie on the ground in a heap feigning some sort of injury – and called on the club physio.

'Have you got any Ralgex?' he asked the physio.

Ralgex, for those of you who haven't ever inhaled in a rugby changing room, is a pungent ointment smeared on aching muscles with a strangely warming effect. It can sting a bit, especially when applied to sensitive areas. Deep Heat is another well-known brand. Graham took a large dollop and smeared it all over his ear. For some strange reason, after the next scrum, his opposite number was squawking and squealing in pain and desperately calling for some water to wash his mouth out.

I was glad to be alongside someone with Graham's experience for my first encounter with a French front row. However, I was less glad to be sleeping alongside someone who snored like a chorus of elephant seals warming up for an international yodelling competition. The decibel level had probably been nudged up a bit by the copious quantities of alcohol that had been consumed on the journey. As I lay awake with Fieldy's nocturnal sound waves rearranging my internal organs, I began to worry that he might hit on our hotel's resonant frequency and bring the building down in a heap, killing us all.

It was not the best preparation for my first international encounter, but after a breakfast of coffee and croissants I boarded the team coach for the Parisian suburbs and the Stade Français training ground. For many of the club's older social members this is their one game of the season, so the changing room was full of ageing gentlemen squeezing their limbs into tubes of neoprene, pulling moth-eaten remnants of kit out of their bags, discreetly trying to stretch off infrequently used muscles and negotiating for a smaller role in the fixture.

I was going to have to wait for my chance to get onto the pitch because the person generally organising things was Tim Lunn, a fellow hooker and someone way above me in the pecking order as a former 1st-team captain and tour veteran of many years standing. He would inevitably bagsy the space in the middle of the scrum. This was probably just as well. For all the friendly pre-match bonhomie, the physical nature of this fixture looked a notch or two up from the pootling encounters I had been used to.

The home side were in considerably better shape than our lot and it didn't take long for some of our ageing, unfit and hung-over players to retire and create a space for me on the pitch. Very kind of them, of course, and I was naturally immensely grateful for the opportunity to be generally roughed up in a Gallic accent for the rest of the game.

I puffed out my chest and jogged onto the pitch with Elgar's *Pomp and Circumstance* playing in my head and a surge of red-blooded patriotism pumping through my veins. I tucked myself in at the back of a scrum and prepared to shove the next scrum as hard as I could.

The French seemed to play a different style of rugby to anything I had been used to: aggressive and niggly. I found myself in the midst of a maul and for the first time realised why that part of the game had been given that name. I was being severely mauled by a Gaul. Someone had decided to tenderise this small cut of *rosbif* by thumping it in the ribs, twisting my limbs under my body and taking my head off as if to prepare me for the oven.

It was as though the French were going out of their way to provoke a reaction, goading us to respond, trying to pick a fight. It certainly worked. At one point, after being pushed and pulled about more than I thought was really necessary, I stroppily tore myself free and puffed myself up to my full 5 foot 6 inches, ready to confront whoever's arm it was that had been wrapped round my neck. Unfortunately, that turned out to have been an enormous second-row forward. As I sheepishly backed down, he grinned toothlessly at me and gave me a playful pat on the side of the head, temporarily deafening me in the process.

I hung on in the game for as long as possible, just about managing to hook a few balls back in the scrum and occasionally managing to find one of our players when I threw in at the line-out. The rest of the time I was just trying to survive without being broken in two. The French were scoring lots of tries and on the rare occasion when we did get the ball we were dropping lots of passes. One of our backs was as a result renamed Edward Scissorhands. Fortunately, no one seemed to be keeping score and at last the game reached a natural conclusion once everyone had had enough of a run-out. Gallic shrugs and English nods and winks turned to handshakes and we all headed for the changing rooms.

Then the party really started. Our changing rooms and the training pitch may have been a bit rough and ready, but the lunch laid on there by our hosts was first class. Tables heaving with huge bowls of pâté, cheeses and pickles were laid out alongside the pitch along with big sacks full of baguettes. It was all washed down with copious quantities of red wine. The cry *'saucissons!'* went up and massive trays of thick, spicy, barbequed sausages were brought round. Having been comprehensively duffed up on the pitch, we were now being treated to the warmest hospitality by the most charming group of men you could ever hope to meet.

Affectionate presentations and toasts were made with senior players from both sides speaking in the other nation's language. Gifts including club ties, T-shirts and a large cheese were exchanged and promises were made to meet again in Warlingham in a year's time. Feeling full of fine food and lots of *entente cordiale* we bundled onto the coach and made our way back into the city for the next stage of the tour.

Our hosts had sorted out tickets for us for the international but that was not until late in the evening, so we still had an afternoon to kill. We set off for a serious pub crawl across the city, and somehow or other I became the kitty master. This meant that I had the money and as a result the alcoholics were never far away. As we weaved from bar to bar, small groups of Frenchmen in blue tops would burst into song as they spotted our England shirts and we exchanged a bit of good-natured banter. We had made the mistake of drinking the ridiculously overpriced and overcarbonated French beer. With a dwindling kitty and bloated bellies we opted for a change of game plan. The final hour before the game was spent sitting at tables on the pavement outside a bar, knocking back a few bottles of red wine and admiring the stunning Parisian beauties that wandered past.

This city was very romantic after all. I was now deeply in love with France, the French and even with the drunken and dishevelled bunch of reprobates I was travelling with. As I walked into the packed French national stadium, lit up for the evening international fixture, and fizzing with centuries of Anglo-French rivalry, I stood there breathing in the atmosphere and realised that I was of course in love with rugby too. To top it all the men in white comprehensively beat *Les Bleus* in a thrilling match and I returned to the UK fired up and inspired and looking forward even more to the next 4th-XV fixtures.

Chapter 11

Captain's Poker

Focus, Discipline, Leadership. A Commitment to Excellence. Striving for 110 per cent. Setting Goals and Sticking to Them. These are all buzzwords and phrases that had little or nothing at all to do with my approach to captaincy of the 4th XV.

I imagine it is vaguely possible that corporate management jargon, advanced sports psychology and the occasional isotonic energy drink may have helped the England national side beat France in the other fixture that was played during my weekend in Paris. However, in the lowly 4ths, over my first season in charge I discovered that there is a more subtly nuanced set of attributes that are required for sporting success.

The first basic principle is: the fewer players you have to draw upon, the less likely you are to win. This is not really a problem for the English national rugby selectors who, at the last count, have around two million registered players to choose from and can normally rustle up fifteen stout-hearted chaps and as many replacement players as the rules will allow to start a game without much difficulty. Down in the 4th XV it was a major triumph to have got the numbers on my team sheet into double figures by the Tuesday evening when the club circular went to press.

At the selection meeting with the other team captains and club coaches, I had to be very careful how I described my chances of getting a side out at the weekend, and play my cards very close to my chest. On Tuesday evenings in the club's committee room a five-day-long game of 'Captains' Hold 'em Poker' begins. The rules are as follows:

First the club manager deals out cards with the players' names on to each of the captains. Unlike normal poker he deals the first fifteen to the 1st-team captain, the second fifteen to the 2nd-team captain and so on. The 4th-team captain gets whatever cards are left at the end. The 1st-team captain will then 'see' players in the other sides that he likes the look of and take them. He may possibly 'discard' a few of his own cards of players he knows are injured, working or likely to be arrested for being drunk and disorderly on the Friday night. Players are swapped and shuffled around until one team has less than ten players. That team then 'folds' i.e. cancels its game, and the other captains then scrabble around to grab the players for their own team.

The only way to succeed at Captains' Poker from the 4th-team seat is to have approximately ten players on the table, who are known to be worse than useless. All the other captains then feel able to ignore these. Meanwhile you need to have another stack of players up your sleeve that no one else knows about, who have declared their availability only to you. You then need to smuggle them into the clubhouse, if necessary wearing sunglasses and a false beard, about five minutes before the kick-off.

If you don't have any other players up your sleeve, then you need to pull off a serious 'bluff'. This is to convince not just the other captains, but also the club administrators that you will still somehow manage to get a side out and honour the fixture. You also need to convince the very few players that have ended up in your side that it will be worth their while turning up. If they get a sniff of the possibility that you might be short of numbers and they will either end up playing in three positions simultaneously or the game as a whole will be scrapped, then they may go and find something better to do with their Saturday afternoon.

In the later rounds of the game a new pack of player cards are introduced one by one over the next few days, any time up to about half an hour before the kick-off, as a few disorganised club members and friends of members turn up looking for a game. Captains then compete to lure the new players into their sides by offering preferred playing positions, promises of post-match alcohol and possible sexual favours. During this phase of the game, teams with away fixtures are at a distinct disadvantage as they will need to be on the road and out of the poker game an hour or so earlier than anyone else.

In a further complication, you have to remember that other clubs will also be playing their own version of Captains' Poker and every now and again one of your opponents' sides will cry off their game as they run out of players. This leads to another unseemly scramble to snaffle up the players left kicking their heels before they are dragged off to IKEA by their wives and girlfriends.

Just to confuse matters further, the playing cards have minds of their own and will occasionally decide that they are no longer available to play for the captain to whom they have been dealt, having developed a mysterious injury, work commitment or terminal hangover.

And so I have as 4th-team captain at various points in my career started a game with fifteen keen beans on the pitch and a further fifteen on the touchline, changed, warmed up and stretched off, eager to get on. On other days I have been at an away fixture hiding in a changing room minutes before the scheduled kick-off with barely ten or eleven players, most of whom can only manage twenty minutes of a game at best before collapsing from exhaustion.

However, whatever hand I had been dealt, I made it a point of principle never to turn away a potential player, and never to cry off a fixture. Away matches were always the hardest to recruit players for but if the worst came to the worst, I would take whatever number of players I had with me and try and make the best of a bad job. When I travelled to Croydon for our return fixture later in the season, I had a very bad job indeed of which to make the best.

Croydon Rugby Club play a little way south of the concrete jungle of office blocks and flyovers, in an area called Shirley.

They have one private pitch, which seems to rely on liberal applications of knee-grazing sand to keep it level every season. However, our fixture was to be played on the public playing fields on the other side of a fast, straight stretch of road whose high rate of accidents and fatalities has earned it the nickname of the Mad Mile. Once you have changed you have to negotiate the traffic and cross the busy road, which can be more difficult than it sounds. For my team, containing several arthritic pensioners, slipping and sliding on the tarmac road in metal-studded boots turned out to be quite a perilous warm-up.

The Croydon 2nd-team pitch has the unique attraction of a slope upwards at both ends being set in a valley that is not quite wide enough or flat enough. Added to that, a colony of moles has usually been up all night building a small housing complex in one corner of the pitch and there are an inevitable couple of little piles of unscooped dog poop. So perhaps it is not surprising that, in spite of spending the entire week making frantic phone calls and bombarding players with text messages and emails, I could only drag thirteen players out onto our opponents' pitch.

Croydon, meanwhile, had amassed about twenty-seven players and they had been warming up and familiarising themselves with the moley topology for about an hour. Having lost to us at our home ground earlier in the season, they were looking for revenge.

My team may have been barely in double figures but our average age was almost into three figures.

For once, Dr Glover wasn't the oldest in our side. Peter Braithwaite, the silver-haired chartered surveyor and Parisian tour organiser, had been persuaded to join us and was gently warming up for a run-out on the wing. The experienced Bob Nunn had forsaken the opportunity to watch his son playing for the 1st team and was ready to join me in the front row.

In a last-minute negotiation with Warlingham's 3rd-team captain, I had managed to secure the services of another young multi-purpose forward called Ben. This may have been due to the fact that he was not thought to have washed his kit or body for at least three seasons and was universally accepted to be the smelliest person you could ever share a scrum with. He was in a very grumpy mood as a result of being dropped, but fortunately directed his frustrations at the opposition players.

Even though I had only thirteen players, with Ben having something to prove in the pack and a few of the Clapham boys running around in the backs, we found ourselves two tries up after only twenty minutes. Something about going into battle so clearly outnumbered had fired up the testosterone, adrenalin and maybe even the Steradent levels in our team and we were playing out of our socks. Croydon's players meanwhile, worn out after an excessive warm-up, were then subjected to an increasingly bad-tempered and incomprehensible stream of abuse from their own captain.

Unfortunately, it wasn't to last. As we started to wilt, Croydon regrouped. The Clapham hangovers kicked in and the Steradent stimulant properties wore off. Croydon spotted the gaping holes in our defences and passed the ball to some tiny but speedy players who ran through our lines several times to score a succession of easy tries. Still, we stuck at it, dropped a forward from scrum into the backs and managed to pick up another couple of tries of our own. Players who had only been planning a gentle run-out for twenty minutes or so kept going for the full eighty and at the end of the game, the few of us that had made the journey to Shirley mole sanctuary were glad we had. I was happy to have got enough players onto the pitch to be competitive and I had even won a couple of scrums against the head.

There was a similar pattern throughout the season; I managed to get a side out for all our league fixtures but getting a win was proving to be more of a challenge. We'd had the odd victory but most of our league points were just for turning up. In the lower divisions of the Surrey RFU league structure, sides are awarded two points for simply presenting themselves for a fixture with more than ten players. If a side fails to appear for a game or cries off, walkover points are allocated to the other side. As a result, without really winning much, we still had more points than a couple of other sides in the league by virtue of the fact that we had made it to more games than them.

For me it was a minor victory every week to have played my hand well enough in the rounds of Captains' Poker and to have managed to get close to fifteen players onto a pitch for each of our league fixtures. As a result thirty or so fat blokes got a bit of a runaround, a break from the routine and a chance to unwind over a pint or two afterwards. I was probably doing more for the health and general well-being of those men, their families and work colleagues than I had ever managed in any of my earnest and well-intentioned professional and political activities.

The 4th XV had gained a little momentum and a bit of a reputation for being an agreeable place to spend a Saturday afternoon. We were officially the third-worst side in Surrey, but I embraced the title and used it to recruit new players nervous about playing at too competitive a level. We picked up additional friendly fixtures from clubs who wanted to see if we were really that bad and organised a charity fund-raising game against the dads who coached the Warlingham junior and mini sides.

Our final league fixture of the season was against the Sutton and Epsom 6th XV. Quite a lot of our opponents seemed to have been from paired places (Streatham and Croydon, Croydon and Shirley Wanderers, Purley and John Fisher), as a result of club mergers that had happened over the years. Clearly the merger had been successful for Sutton and Epsom as they now seemed to be able to turn out six sides regularly, though one might have thought that if things were going that well they could demerge and create two healthy clubs with three sides each, three in Epsom and three in Sutton.

With their six sides, Sutton and Epsom are too big for their own ground somewhere halfway between the two Surrey commuter towns. When we had travelled to visit them earlier in the season, we had to change at their clubhouse and then all get back into our cars and find a playing field a couple of miles away in a nearby sixth-form college. Getting fifteen dozy blokes to navigate to one place on a Saturday afternoon is hard enough, without adding in an additional treasure hunt to get to the pitch. As a result we were entirely disorganised and unprepared for the fixture, which, unsurprisingly, we lost.

For the return match I was a little more prepared. Our fixture was the only home game in the club that weekend and so I had the pick of the players who had turned up on the off chance looking for a game. The university Easter holidays had also just started so there were a handful of students lurking around, all keen for a run-out.

The mood throughout the club as a whole was very buoyant as the 1st team had secured the top spot in their league and were celebrating their promotion. The bar was busy and a little crowd of supporters was assembling to watch our fixture. Our league, Surrey Combination 4, was still competitive in the last weekend of the season and Sutton and Epsom were one of four clubs within two points of each other at the top of the table. A win against us would secure them the title.

In spite of the availability of an abundance of potential ringers on the touchline, refugees from higher sides with nothing better to do, I started the game with my 4th-team regulars. People like John Glover, Mark Garner and Robin Ellingham, who had turned out for me regularly throughout the season and had earned their place on the field with loyalty and reliability. The slightly less reliable but none the less loyal Clapham boys had also turned up and secured their places in the starting line-up.

After a little burst of early pressure we somehow managed to secure a penalty in front of the posts. Clapham boy and city banker Ben Hathaway had made the glamour role of fly half his own during the season and he tidily kicked the ball through the posts to get us into the lead against the league leaders.

For the next twenty minutes something magical happened. For once the 4th XV seemed to gel. We scored three quick tries including one from John Burrell, who had given me that beautifully timed pass earlier in the season that had led to my only proper try. It seemed that we could score at will from anywhere on the pitch, with a prop and a winger each picking up five points. Each try was followed by a tidy conversion from Ben.

Sutton and Epsom fought back hard, camping inside our twenty-two for a sustained period at the end of the half but our rock-solid defence kept them from being able to get over the try line. A comfortable margin at half-time allowed me to give some of my old-timers a well-earned rest and bring on some of the students and other hangers-on who were lurking on the touchline. Everyone had some fun with daring runs and silly passes, but more tries followed and our lead grew. My little 4th XV, cobbled together on a wing and a prayer every week, had somehow managed to overturn the league leaders. We were not only going to win but we were going to win in style. We had a team with strength, spirit and even a few regular supporters. As we wandered back to the changing rooms after finishing our last game of the season as comfortable winners, I felt proud, inspired and utterly delighted.

The Warlingham 1st team might have been League Champions but I felt in the 4s we had accomplished something just as important. We had created a side out of next to nothing, turned up and made several great games of rugby possible. A group of old blokes, city boys and students had become something beginning to resemble a team. Whatever else was happening in the rest of our lives, on a Saturday afternoon everything just seemed to work and rugby had made it happen.

I reassured the men in blazers that I would be delighted to continue as captain of the 4th XV next season, and retreated with a real sense of achievement for the summer to reacquaint myself with the family, my career and the rest of life outside the happy confines of Warlingham Rugby Club.

Chapter 12

Cuddles, Ramadan and Hamish

A work colleague of mine had a theory that the perfect length of time to stay in any job was three years. One year to work out how to do the job, one year doing it and the third year to apply for your next one. I had singularly failed to apply this strategy in my professional career and had been lurching from one job to another rather too rapidly. I thought I would try a more steady approach with my rugby. Three seasons seemed the right number to aim for, and in season two the job of captaining the 4th XV got a little easier and even more enjoyable.

We turned up at Croydon once again for our away fixture

with barely a dozen players. This time, I swallowed my pride and asked to borrow a couple of their players to make it a more even and competitive game. Croydon generously lent us two spares including a prop called Cuddles. Cuddles was, as you might imagine, a generously proportioned gentleman, whose teeth didn't seem to quite fit in his head. Round, balding, probably in his late forties or early fifties, we had exchanged a good deal of front-row banter in previous fixtures. Having a good nickname had helped us to remember him and he was welcomed to our ranks.

The pre-match exchange of players is one of the best aspects of rugby at this sort of level. Some time before the kick-off the two captains will seek each other out for a genuinely friendly introduction. Even though we are about to pitch our respective sides into a brutal physical encounter, we will chat like old friends and endeavour to even up any unseemly imbalances between the two sides.

It is quite hard to imagine professional captains doing anything similar. They would presumably be too busy working with team psychologists to get themselves into a strange place known only as 'The Zone'. At best, opposing professional captains will exchange a brief handshake and a hard stare. If there are ever friendly exchanges between serious sporting captains they might occur at the end of a fixture, the end of a season or at the end of their careers when they are reunited under the watchful eye of Sue Barker on *A Question of Sport*.

Rugby captains on the lower rungs of the game know that they have both just been engaged in an exhausting struggle, far more draining than anything about to happen on the pitch, just to get something approaching fifteen disorganised, dishevelled and often mentally impaired individuals into the clubhouse, changed and onto the pitch. Any local authority social services department charged with the same task would probably send a small army of care workers, special needs assistants and drivers equipped with disability aids, hoists and sundry adaptations and still struggle to get them onto the field of play. Before a game, it is always a pleasure to meet the one person who knows what you have just been through to get there.

Although both captains are always keen to win, the result of any one match is never the be-all and end-all. Getting everyone a decent game is just as important, as is the longer-term relationship between the two clubs. No one really enjoys a lopsided mismatch. If you are running in one try after another against a demoralised opposition there is a rapidly diminishing marginal rate of return for every point accumulated. Handing over a few players or in desperate situations swapping a few round at half-time keeps everyone happy and the game competitive. Being a good host and a good guest also helps to keep the fixtures in the calendar and honoured every year. Without strong, healthy local teams to play against, no club can survive.

So with Cuddles in our front row we were able to play contested scrums and everyone seemed to be happy. Apart, that is, from one of the Croydon second row. Gradually, throughout the game, the level of animosity between our temporary transferee and his club comrades seemed to grow out of all proportion with the rest of the game. Niggles and mutterings were exchanged between them that none of the Warlingham players could comprehend. Cuddles turned distinctly uncuddly and ended up in a full-on scrap with a Croydon second-row player. Our little captains' pre-match arrangement had given an opportunity for some old Croydon scores to be settled. We left them to sort it out amongst themselves and eventually the game restarted with none of my team any the wiser as to what it had all been about.

It wasn't the first time that I had seen how lending players to the opposition can have quite an effect on the players donated. Quite often during our home fixtures, John Glover would find himself in a different-coloured shirt. Being a little older than most of my players, he wasn't always my first choice for the starting line-up. Being a little more mature, he was also less likely to have a hissy fit, unlike some of the teenagers, if asked to play for the other side. John has been around long enough to understand that the game as a whole is more important than any one team-selection decision on any given Saturday afternoon.

Unfortunately, John had an annoying habit of playing significantly better for the opposition than he ever did for us. A confident and likeable communicator, he would quickly chat up the other side and get himself in a good position to set up a cheeky switch pass or some other fancy move dredged up from his long rugby-playing history. He would always rather get a full game than shiver on the touchline, but something about being considered dispensable enough to be given a free transfer to the opposition motivated him just that little bit more to show us all that there was life in the old dog yet.

Of course we lost to Croydon, even with Cuddles picking off the opposition with his private battles, but we strengthened the growing bond between the two clubs and would look forward to the return fixture later in the season. A few weeks later we picked up a home win against the team from the opposite side of the concrete jungle, Streatham and Croydon. That, however, was more down to the fact that their captain, Abdul, was celebrating Ramadan and as a result had to get through the entire game without a single mouthful of water or a half-time orange segment. He was exhausted, drained and dehydrated but devoutly declined all our offers of a glug from a water bottle throughout the game.

In this my second, consolidation season, I also began to get a little better at another aspect of the game: dealing with referees.

Rugby can find a role for almost every body shape and personality in one position or another somewhere in a team. The very few that can't be found a place in a team can always become referees. Referees are the most diverse group of any within the game, with widely divergent behaviour and interpretation of the rules. Without them no game of rugby would be possible, however, and their unpredictability helps to make the game endlessly entertaining.

Down in the lower leagues, there are never quite enough proper referees to go around. As a result, the men and women who are press-ganged into officiating offer such a varied approach to the game that you almost end up playing an entirely different sport every week.

Senior sides in higher leagues will normally be granted the honour of having a 'Society' referee take charge of their games. This does not necessarily mean that the man with whistle is a cousin of the fourteenth Earl of Tofftonshire, just about to dash off in his Jag with Lady Annabel to the polo. No, instead it means that they have somehow found time in their otherwise empty lives to spend two or three evenings in a draughty school hall being clicked through a faded PowerPoint presentation about experimental law variations and the best way to tuck a pencil into your socks. By demonstrating superhuman degrees of nerdiness, they are admitted to their local county Society of Rugby Football Union Referees and may henceforth be referred to as 'Society Refs'.

Understandably there are not many people who are prepared to go through the process of joining a society where the only perk of membership would appear to be a begrudged pint of warm beer once a week, after having been sworn and shouted at by thirty players and assorted spectators for eighty minutes on a Saturday afternoon. Only those condemned to spend their weekends visiting garden centres or in-laws might consider this to be a pleasure or a privilege.

So for every thirty people who can be found to play a game of rugby, one more needs to be found to adjudicate on the laws and minimise the bloodshed. Every club needs to find a member who can be called upon to take up the whistle with or without the official training. Warlingham has come up with some real treats.

After a few games at home at Warlingham, it gradually became apparent to me that we had someone very special in our resident club referee, who we shall refer to as Hamish McKilt. I should be clear here that I mean 'special' as in 'needs'. Hamish was an irascible Scotsman who appeared to take absolutely no pleasure in refereeing whatsoever. From his first utterance on the pitch to his last grumblings in the bar, everything that he had to deal with was so unimaginably wrong that one began to wonder why he ever took up the sport or indeed life at all.

Hamish saw it as his duty to enforce levels of deference and obedience that would make a Soho dominatrix blush. Penalties and punishments were awarded almost entirely at random and almost always in favour of the home side. The slightest complaint, muttering or indeed quizzical expression would be instantly met by advancing the other side 10 yards or a sending-off. He is the only person I have ever known penalise someone for 'running too fast', or indeed 'looking at me like that. You know what you're doing. Yes, you.'

Very occasionally Hamish went the extra mile to ensure harmony on the pitch. In one game we were playing a side called London French. There are a number of sides in London with historical links to other countries or counties, including London Cornish and London Irish. Many others have links to schools and universities. But with falling player numbers most clubs will take anyone who wants to play regardless of nationality or old school tie. London French's lower side didn't appear to have any French players whatsoever but Hamish refused to acknowledge this aberration. He took great pains to offer his judgements and rulings in both English and very poor sub O-level French. As his grumpiness grew throughout the game and his angry Glaswegian/

Gallic instructions grew louder and louder, he ended up shouting violently in fluent Franglais at the opposition captain:

'Penalty pour les mains dans le ruck... Retournez dix metres maintenant or else c'est le sin bin pour vous.'

Eventually the London French skipper replied, 'I've no idea what you are saying, mate, I'm from Fulham.'

Other clubs have exacted their revenge by fielding referees of equal randomness and unpredictability. However, all of them, with all their faults, have still enabled thirty or more overweight and unfit men to burn off some calories and fend off heart disease for perhaps a year or two. They may not share a common understanding of the rules of the game but that shouldn't really matter. As most of the players have never read or learnt the rules, it seems to me to be of entirely secondary importance for the referees to know them either. If a referee does the basic job of blowing a whistle at the beginning and end of each game and telling you why you lost over a pint afterwards in the bar, then that's enough for me. Hamish's quirky refereeing became one of the regular features of many of our home games. Against Chobham he excelled himself.

We had been comprehensively beaten by Chobham when we had visited their even more upmarket and leafy corner of Surrey earlier in the season. The long journey and lush surroundings had unsettled and intimidated my players and we had half-expected to be greeted by the butler as we arrived at their club. We had one brief moment early in the first half when we might just possibly have got some points onto the scoreboard. With the advantage of going downhill we had ended up contesting a line-out close to their try line. With a nice light teenager to throw up in the air, we managed to win the ball from the defending team's throw-in.

Unfortunately, the ball was then popped down to me standing just behind the line-out, close to the touchline. Normally I can stand here and catch my breath without having to do a great deal. The opposition can normally be relied on to secure the ball and either form a little maul amongst themselves or pass the ball out to their backs. This time, however, the ball had fallen neatly into my hands and it took a little while to get over the shock and consider what to do next. Should I perhaps run round the back of the line and build up a little momentum for a run towards the try line? Should I put my head down and drive straight forward up the narrow channel along the touchline and try and find a way through there? Perhaps I could head towards my own pack and set up a rolling maul or maybe even pass the ball directly to our scrum half for him to set up something with the backs. The possibilities were endless but my indecision was of course fatal. As I dithered momentarily, the opposition pack pounced on me from all angles and bundled me unceremoniously into touch, rearranging my limbs and internal organs in the process. We ended up losing by lots to nil.

So, on their return trip a few weeks later to the slightly cheaper end of Surrey, the Chobham team were quite reasonably expecting to win once again. They hadn't counted on Hamish's extraordinary refereeing style.

From the start Hamish awarded us penalty after penalty for unfathomable offences, helping our pack to make steady progress up the field. Any Chobham protest, complaint or slightly raised eyebrow would result in the penalty being moved 10 yards further up the pitch. As Chobham scratched their heads, trying to work out what possible offence they could have committed, our forwards, who were now broadly familiar with Hamish's approach to officiating, took quick tap penalties to keep up the momentum. A few quick passes between the forwards and our prop John Waghorn ran over the line to score the first try.

Chobham quickly worked out that there was no point arguing with the referee and that the best way to make sure we didn't win any penalties was to make sure we didn't get the ball. They worked the ball back up into the final quarter of the pitch and in spite of Hamish's best efforts stayed there, launching attack after attack. Eventually one of them made it over the try line and clearly grounded the ball. Hamish, however, saw it differently and declared that the ball had been held up over the line i.e. suggesting that one of our side had somehow squeezed a bit of their anatomy between the ball and the grass before the attacking side could ground it. Of course the referee is always right in rugby, even when he is wrong, so I could only conclude that someone must indeed have dropped a contact lens onto the turf just where the ball had been placed, preventing the points from being awarded.

Chobham, resigned to their fate, gave up worrying about the score and continued to absorb our referee-assisted attacks for the rest of the game, without bothering unduly to try and score again for themselves. We managed just one more try as our token ringer from the 2nd team ran the entire width of the pitch, offering each of our backs in turn a switch pass and a try-winning opportunity. A switch pass is where two backs running at different angles pass the ball between them, changing the direction of play and confusing the opposition. This, however, was only serving to confuse our more simple-minded backs and so they all watched on bemused as the ringer went off and scored the try himself instead.

There are rarely any bad feelings left after a game, even one as ridiculous as this. Both sides know that the score doesn't really matter. No one will be splashed all over the back page of the tabloids the following morning. Even the local press would struggle to find space or the inclination to cover the activities of a few wheezing and arthritic alcoholics and an utterly random referee. We could all safely retreat to the bar, share a jug or two of beer and negotiate any moral victories we could care to claim. There might have been a battle and there were inevitably a few scars, but we would all live to fight another day on another field with, hopefully, an alternative referee.

Referee management aside, the eighty minutes of the game were the easiest part of the role of being a captain. It gave me a chance to have a little rest before embarking on the post-match rituals.

Leading the men on the field of play is far less important a task than dealing with the club officials off the pitch afterwards. As soon as I made it into the bar, an agitated Chair of the Equipment and Facilities and General Tediousness Subcommittee would seek me out and hassle me to collect match subscriptions from all the players, along with securing their availability for the following week. This particular club official also suffered from a rare form of OCD concerning the whereabouts of the balls, water bottles and shirts. Rugby balls go missing at an alarming rate, kicked into bushes around the pitch and lost forever or scooped up by opposing teams as legitimate spoils of war. I had a particular problem with water bottles, which seemed to grow legs and wander off in search of better-quality players to rehydrate. Just when I wanted to slump in a corner and recuperate with a nice cup of tea and a plate of chips I would need to shake down all the players and relieve them of fivers and any club kit that they had accidentally put in their own bags.

A bag of twenty club shirts tends to dwindle over the course of a season. Younger players apparently like to snaffle a shirt at the end of a game as a trophy or memento of their selection in the squad. They drift from club to club, through school and university sides, quietly accumulating 'stash' as a mark of their successful rugby-playing career. The more stash you have, the better a player you apparently are. Older players blaming a combination of Alzheimer's and concussion might mistakenly pack the odd muddy shirt away in their kitbag out of habit or filch one just to prove to their wives that they were at the rugby club rather than having an affair.

Sets of shirts normally start life with the 1st team, shiny and new with a sponsor's logo prominently displayed across the chest. As two or three go missing, the set is dropped down to the 2nd team. More go AWOL and what's left is handed down to the 3s. As the colour begins to fade and the stripes of different colour merge into one shade of grubby grey, the remnants of two or three sets of shirts will be amalgamated and dumped outside the local Oxfam shop. The 4th-team captain then has to go and reclaim them in the dead of night to kit out his lowly side. I would regularly send out teams with three players each wearing a different number 20 shirt and John Glover wearing his own shirt in the totally different colours that Warlingham played in before the last war. We haven't yet had to use body paint to apply club colours to someone's naked torso but it has got pretty close.

Shirts go missing for the oddest of reasons. At the end of one game, a young Irish front-row player called Ciaran sat on the bench in the changing room and didn't seem to be showing any signs of getting changed. I had been pleased to get him out on the pitch that afternoon. He had recently acquired a girlfriend after a long stint of being single, so I was worried we might lose him as his new lady friend introduced him to the delights of shopping in Croydon on a Saturday afternoon, putting up shelves and mowing lawns. But no, fortunately he seemed keen to play and apparently his girlfriend was keen for him to play also.

As I was collecting up the shirts, Ciaran started to look a little sheepish. Quietly under his breath he asked if he could hang onto his shirt for a couple of days. It turns out that the new love in his life was rather keen that he make his way straight home after the game, without showering or changing out of his kit. The sight of her young man still steaming in a hot, sweaty, mud-and-blood-encrusted rugby shirt was, I was told, all that was needed to inflame this young woman's passions and a torrid night of energetic and imaginative lovemaking was guaranteed.

I wished him the best of luck, left him with the shirt and promised that we would keep this little arrangement between ourselves. Quite how the rest of the club found out so quickly I can't imagine.

Chapter 13

A Drinking Club with a Rugby Problem

Rugby at all levels is associated in most people's minds with drinking and indeed drinking very heavily. The popular image of rugby players is of boorish misogynists spending long nights in the clubhouse, consuming vast quantities of alcohol and then doing unspeakable things involving digestive biscuits and bodily fluids. Extreme drunkenness amongst rugby players and fans is also thought to remove inhibitions and expose some pretty extreme, reactionary views. Polly Toynbee of *The Guardian* fame wrote that dropping a bomb on Twickenham during a rugby international would set back the cause of fascism in this country for several generations.

As if the violent physical contact, intimate male on male grappling and risk of personal injury on the pitch wasn't enough, rugby seems to have gone out of its way to create a culture off the pitch that is even more aggressive and likely to involve a trip to A & E. Perhaps more than the on-field hazards, the post-match antics put many people off getting involved in the sport and seriously affect the way they think about those who do take part. The reality of course is somewhat different. Rugby players and supporters are no better or worse than any other segment of society. I play and drink with people who vote for all political parties and none. The only extremities that are normally exposed are kept to the post-match showers or the communal bath.

It will come as a surprise, perhaps, that it was often quite a struggle to get my 4th team to bond over a post-match beer or two. With players drawn from widely different generations and walks of life, once we got off the pitch and changed, natural male reticence would kick in and players drifted to different corners of what is quite a large clubhouse and then drifted fairly swiftly to their different corners of Croydon and Surrey. The 1st-team boys, being a slightly more homogeneous group, would often stay and drink a little more, but quite often they too would soon quietly slip away to their homes, wives or girlfriends and settle down in front of *The X Factor* like the rest of the population. The 2nd team were a little better and went with the motto 'Win or lose, we booze.'

As I tried to get the 4th-team post-match boozing started, a few of the teenagers in the team would hover around me as I approached the bar. Like flies circling around a recently collapsed tramp they could sniff out the possibility of free drink from forty paces. Affectionately known as the Inbetweeners, because of their uncanny resemblance to the characters in the situation comedy and hit film, the kids like Kieran, Ben, Chris and Joe would sidle up to me as I got my wallet out and see if they could extract a pint of Strongbow or a luminous alcopop from me. Keen to retain their playing services the following week I would usually oblige until I ran out of money. They all, I assume, regarded it as a badge of honour to never be seen buying a round themselves.

I didn't begrudge them the odd scrounged drink. The Inbetweeners were a welcome and entertaining feature of the team. These were young men who had come up through the mini and junior ranks of the club and were keen to break into the senior game. They were all rather good little players but slightly too young, green and breakable to be included in the higher sides. With the 4th XV they got a regular run-out against older, heavier and slower players and a chance to test out their recently discovered adult bodies in an adult game of rugby.

Every week they would heroically drag themselves out of bed at the crack of lunchtime, pile into Ben's car, a typical teenager's beaten-up, barely insurable, second-hand hatchback, and make their way to the club. If we were playing away then we would assemble a little convoy of cars and make our way over to places like Merton or Kingston. As I kept an eye on Ben in my rear-view mirror I would often see a car full of teenagers headbanging to 'Bohemian Rhapsody' like the stars of *Wayne's World*, with great clouds of cigarette smoke pouring out of all the windows and vents.

Occasionally we would lose them as they took a diversion to pick up a McFlurry and fries or some extra supplies of Haribo, but they always found us in the end and made their way onto the pitch. Full of teenage bravado, they would all haggle before the kick-off to try and secure their favoured position. Each would wax lyrical about his own sporting prowess and describe in detail the weaknesses of his supposed mates. Then on the pitch they would last about five minutes before being flattened by a marauding opponent and hobbling off to the touchline in search of nicotine and Red Bull.

The great thing about these boys was that they didn't have to play rugby or do any sport at all. As far as I could tell there were no obvious pushy parents on the touchline or careers advisors urging them onto the field in search of interesting things to include in their university application forms. They could have stayed at home on their sofas eating Pringles and playing with their Xbox or frantically pleasuring themselves over X-rated websites. They could have no doubt got up to all sorts of mischief and presumably they did much of the time, but once a week they would pull themselves into a rugby shirt, grow up a bit and play a big part in our team. The grown-ups in the side might not have been perfect role models for them, but there is no doubt we played a small part in helping to turn these slightly dodgy little boys into half-decent young men.

The link between beer and rugby is strong and I have a theory that it is something to do with the reason I took up the game in the first place and the reason that I stuck with it. When life becomes a bit complicated – work, relationships, money, children, you know the sort of thing – playing rugby is a great way to clear the head. It forces you to stop recircling, recycling and regurgitating the everyday niggles of life in your mind and just deal with the basic physical reality of staying alive on the pitch. And in my experience beer seems to do a similar job.

When IT help desk types can't quite work out why your office computer won't process information any more or how to make the tiny hourglass of doom go away, the standard and almost always successful advice is for you to turn the machine off and turn it back on again. Playing rugby and/or drinking yourself into oblivion seem to me to be not all that dissimilar. Having seven bells knocked out of you on a rugby pitch, and then gently turning your brain off with the aid of increasing levels of alcohol, gives the chance for the mind to reboot. Restarting the old grey matter with the aid of a decent fry-up and a cup of tea on Sunday leaves you ready to process whatever the world has to throw at you on Monday.

Obviously, if drinking yourself into something close to a coma becomes a regular feature of life then there probably is a bigger problem to be dealt with. You might need a new processor, the latest version of the operating system or some more randomly accessible memories. But for the basic problem of having slightly too much going on at any one time, a dual therapy of rugby and beer might once in a while be the right answer. For me, fending off a midlife crisis, once in a while it was. Rather than carrying on self-obsessing about my life, career and relationships, and wondering whether to buy a VW campervan and drive off on my own to Namibia, I would neck a few beers with some delightful chaps and wake up the next afternoon, with little memory as to what had been bothering me the day before.

The worst side effect from post-match beer drinking turned out to be karaoke. I found it very hard to resist the opportunity to share my version of Cab Calloway's 'Minnie the Moocher' or Dolly Parton's 'Stand By Your Man' with anyone who would listen. Fortunately, I also had Dave, my friendly local taxi driver's number programmed into my phone and could always get myself scooped up and delivered home before anyone set me up for a performance of Celine Dion's 'My Heart Will Go On'.

Most of the time, the worst that can happen with alcohol is that someone makes a bit of a fool of themselves. For rugby players that isn't really that much of a disincentive. During a game, as we are crashing around incompetently, working out which way is up and who to pass to, rough and ready rugby players make fools of themselves with alarming regularity. Part of the fun of the game is watching people make mistakes. We have all of course seen each other in the nude in changing rooms, showers and communal baths so we can't really get much more ridiculous by the addition of mere alcohol. Alcohol often simply leads to further harmless entertainment.

On a second tour to Paris, I was lucky enough to share a few drinks with one senior member of the club known as Smudger. Worn down by one too many terms as membership secretary, chasing down subscriptions from evasive players, he was apparently wrestling with a few personal demons by sitting them all down and offering them each a large glass of red wine. By the early evening Smudger was well and truly hammered as others began to make plans to find somewhere nice for dinner. The French tour, as I had discovered, tends to attract the more refined members of the Warlingham fraternity, those who enjoy fine dining and the more sophisticated elements of Parisian nightlife. One of the aesthetes had secured a large table at a good restaurant and we set off through the streets of Paris to find it.

Smudger sadly couldn't walk unaided and attached himself to me for support. As we strolled briskly along the narrow pavements it took all my efforts to keep him from collapsing into the path of a *deux chevaux* or falling into a shop window. His demons meanwhile had enjoyed the aperitif and were looking forward to some more wine with dinner. I needed all my skills as a front-row player to hang onto him and keep him from getting into a fight with every passing Frenchman. We made it to the restaurant eventually but he was so incapable at this point that someone else, a former club coach called Derek, took him back to his hotel.

At this stage things started to get complicated. Smudger knew his room number but couldn't make his room key work. Derek persuaded the hotel to sort him out a new key and dumped him on the bed. This was the right room but sadly in the wrong hotel. The Warlingham party was split over two hotels and Smudger was supposed to be in the other one. When the bed's rightful tenant, Dave Millard, returned later in a jolly mood after an expansive evening enjoying fine wines and agreeable company, he was first confused and then supremely annoyed to find a comatose Smudger snoring and dribbling into his previously so inviting pillow. Unable to rouse or shift him, Dave went off in search of another room key and another bed. Throughout the rest of the night a succession of players would return, tired and emotional, only to find the wrong person in their bed. It was a case of Goldilocks meets Ray Cooney as the bedroom-swapping farce carried on halfway through the night.

The next morning, the cast of characters stumbled one-by-one down to breakfast, each ranting and raving about how their bed had been requisitioned and how they had had to sleep somewhere else, only to be disturbed half an hour later by the next person to return. It took an entertaining hour over coffee and croissants to piece together the sequence of events, get them all reallocated into their rightful rooms and Smudger, still grumpy and confused, harrumphed back to his right hotel.

For every potential rugby recruit put off by the drinking culture, there are plenty more who are drawn to the game because of it. Sadly for us chaps, friends and a social life are sometimes quite hard to come by in the normal run of events. Women seem to be able to strike up long-lasting friendships anywhere and at any time. Men who have relocated for work or study, or to evade the Child Support Agency, sometimes struggle to build a network of friends. Rugby and presumably other sports help to break the ice created by centuries of conditioning and social stereotyping.

The promise of beer and good company drew two young Australians towards the 4th XV. Tom and James were in the UK for their big OE – the obligatory Antipodean 'overseas experience'. They were teaching in a local independent school but came to us in search of some sport and a social life. They turned out to be a godsend and with Tom's ferocious tackling and James' phenomenal pace they started to turn round the fortunes of the third-worst side in Surrey.

Our Aussie additions were also great for morale. We had one miserable away game in Cobham where I had failed to get anything close to fifteen players onto the pitch. Unusually, there were a handful of members of the team who were even more inept at the game than I was. Steven Downes, a sports journalist, was one of them. He had the rare distinction of being shorter and rounder than me. He can write intelligently about the game but without his glasses he couldn't see the ball and if he did get it, couldn't see any of his teammates to pass it to. He was playing, I think, only his second ever game.

The game then went from bad to worse as Steven somehow managed to headbutt and virtually render unconscious one of our few decent players, who had to retire to the touchline with a cluster of cartoon birds tweeting around his head. We fell so far behind that the opposition lent us a couple of players just to try and make a bit more of a game of things.

Even though we had been comprehensively beaten in one of the most humiliating games I have ever played, as we came off the pitch, Tom the Australian beamed at me from under his mop of flame-red hair and declared, 'That was fun!' He had spent the whole game chasing after Cobham players, jumping on them and dragging them to the ground. They would somehow recycle the ball to someone else, as none of us would be anywhere near to support, but Tom would then just get up and hunt down the next person with the ball. Like a ginger ninja, he popped up all over the pitch battling heroically with a never-ending supply of Cobham attackers. Single-handedly he kept our deficit under treble figures, yet at the end he was thanking me for the experience.

So as the season progressed it became apparent that I was going to have to do something to repay the loyalty, energy and enthusiasm of the adventure-seeking and beer-seeking boys and men who were making my Saturday afternoons so enjoyable. We were going to have to have an end-of-season tour and I would have to organise it.

Chapter 14

The 4th-XV Easter Tour

What goes on tour, stays on tour. Sorry.

Chapter 15

To Hellingly and Back

Actually, these days, what goes on tour now goes on Facebook. Sadly, the evidence is already out there on the Internet somewhere. I offer the following in mitigation.

There had been a few Warlingham club expeditions organised since I joined, but I never really felt brave enough to book myself onto any of them and so knew little really of what might be involved. I had picked up vague rumours of dangerously drunken antics involving Eastern European immigration officials and professional ladies who could do extraordinary things with everyday items of sporting equipment. However, the code of tour secrecy remained pretty intact so details and specifics were rarely forthcoming.

So when Big Mal and someone called Ginger offered to underwrite the cost of hiring a coach and driver for my first end-of-season tour with the 4th XV, I wasn't entirely sure what I would be letting myself in for. Big Mal, as the name suggests, fills up a large chunk of the clubhouse bar whenever he is in attendance, with his personality and substantial girth. As well as being generously proportioned, he is also a remarkably generous benefactor to the club. His imposing presence has helped him to carve out a successful career as commercial bailiff and persuasive debt collector. Much of his profit seems to find its way to the cash register behind the bar.

Big Mal clearly expected that by taking care and control of the tour travel arrangements he could ensure mobile mayhem. Knowing nods and winks were broadcast in my direction about the sorts of activities that might follow, but I had no real frame of reference with which to process them. I nervously got on with my task, which was to find an opposition and recruit a touring party.

Warlingham 4th XV had managed to advance to a couple of positions off the bottom of the bottom league in Surrey and so, as I began my search for a suitable opposition, I turned to the Internet to identify the third-worst sides in the neighbouring counties. I didn't want to take the risk of travelling too far in case Big Mal and his coach decided not to bring us home. A scan of the Sussex website revealed that third from the bottom of the bottom league in East Sussex was the Hellingly 2nd XV. I could see from the league table that, like us, they had honoured most of their league fixtures and won a few games but not all of them.

Hellingly is a small village on the A22 close to Eastbourne, the south-coast seaside town. In spite of the latter's distinctly blue-rinse reputation, this qualified in my book as sufficiently adventurous and opened up the possibilities of night-time entertainment suited to the more mature members of the team. It wasn't a terribly arduous journey but it would take us over the county border to a new club that we hadn't played before. What was more, there was a ready-made pun for the tour T-shirts. A quick email exchange with their captain and we had a fixture. Club quartermaster and fellow front-row player John Waghorn designed and commissioned the tour stash consisting of specially embroidered polo shirts and a set of training tops bearing the slogan 'To Hellingly and Back'.

I still wasn't really sure whether I could pull this off. Every week it was still a monumental struggle to get fifteen players together and I had never really managed to facilitate much in the way of post-match bonding. My somewhat reticent bunch of players still seemed to toddle off home fairly quickly after each fixture to their slippers and a cup of cocoa. I needn't have worried, however, as word got around and the seats on the coach were soon booked up. It turned out that quite a lot of people were also looking for the full rugby-club-on-tour experience and were planning to take full advantage of the transport home and not having to worry about drink-driving laws.

The drinking itself started very early with the bar opening up first thing in the morning as we gathered at the clubhouse. The coach was loaded with flagons of cider and bottles of chilli-flavoured vodka. A couple of the more senior players awarded themselves some sort of pseudo-military rank, based on the number of previous tours they had attended, and began issuing arbitrary drinking forfeits for perceived indiscretions and misdemeanours. The coach had barely been travelling for twenty minutes before there were desperate cries for a loo stop, and a coachload of gentlemen with straining bladders lined up in a lay-by behind the coach to relieve themselves.

The singing began shortly after we set off again and the two Aussie boys led us all in a beautiful rendition of Rolf Harris's 'Two Little Boys'. Four-part harmonies were introduced into a chorus involving the unfortunate events following a well-intentioned engineer's efforts to satisfy the physical needs of a sexually demanding wife, until the coach driver hid the microphone. After a stop for lunch and a few beers we rocked up at Hellingly's ground with a little over half an hour before the kick-off.

I appeared to have about thirty players available to play in the match against Hellingly, although I might have been seeing double by this stage. I needed to select a starting line-up but anything remotely strategic or tactical was well beyond me. Instead I gave a position to the first fifteen to make it out of the changing room and onto the pitch in their kit.

There were only three sober players on our side: John Glover; Ben, a relative of Dr Glover's lady friend, who we knew only as Nurse Gladys Emmanuel after the object of Ronnie Barker's affections in the TV series *Open All Hours*; and Tom Osbourne, our scrum half. Tom was entering the first stages of training to become a Methodist minister and had wisely chosen to make his own way to the ground and avoid the alcoholic excesses of the coach. One of the worst affected of the rest was a young prop, known for reasons you can probably imagine as Podge. Paralytic, but keen to start, Podge had managed to get changed quickly enough to be in my initial fifteen. As we kicked off he led the forwards charge and headed at breakneck speed towards the Hellingly player who had caught the ball. Utterly incapable of co-ordinating any part of his body, Podge flew into the first tackle, promptly knocked himself out and became the first player to be substituted after just seven seconds on the pitch.

Not only were we far too drunk to play but we had also made life even more difficult for ourselves by imposing some gratuitous tour rules on the journey down. It being the Easter weekend, each member of the touring party had been given a hard-boiled egg on the coach with instructions to keep it with them at all times. At any stage in the proceedings a member of the tour party could call out 'Easter Bunny' whereupon everyone had to hold their egg aloft. This rule unfortunately still applied during the game. At the first line-out, just as the ball was being thrown in, someone from the touchline shouted out 'Easter Bunny' and every player rummaged around in their shorts, or in some cases in their underpants, to get hold of and display their egg. Meanwhile the Hellingly players picked up the ball and ran off to score some points entirely unopposed.

Gradually we sobered up enough to play more or less a proper game and two or three tries were exchanged between the sides. Hellingly probably won, the referee booked himself up for a course of trauma counselling and we retired to the clubhouse for a few more friendly drinks with our hosts. Club ties and tour T-shirts were exchanged and we enjoyed the early spring sunshine together into the evening.

Beyond this point, however, things get a little hazy. When I say hazy, I mean that in the sense of the total blackout sort of haze. I suspect that the real reason that what goes on tour stays on tour is that no one can really remember what happened. Occasionally I have unsettling flashbacks of human pyramids, desperate dad-dancing and random acts of public nudity. Hypnosis or therapy might uncover more but I'm not sure I ever want to go there. I'm told that Mr and Mrs Big Mal accompanied by Mr and Mrs Smudger had to return to the club the following day to return and replace a few of Hellingly's fixtures and fittings that had somehow found their way back to Surrey.

The only thing I remember clearly is, a few days later, Dave the taxi driver smiling at me when we met in the street and inquiring about my hangover and general well-being. I think he knows too much and he certainly knows more than me. As a result, I now have to book an expensive airport trip with him every two or three months whether or not I am actually travelling anywhere, to secure his ongoing discretion.

None the less I am reliably informed that our mini-tour was a great success. As far as I could tell, no one died or got arrested. The T-shirts are still, to this day, worn with pride around the club by veterans of our Sussex excursion. The 4th team had cemented its status in the club as a side which knew how to enjoy itself even if it couldn't really remember very much about it the next morning. The only problem was that we had one more fixture to honour before the end of the season and only one week to recover. Cranleigh were waiting for us and we were collectively a little unwell.

Chapter 16

Mind Over Matter: If I Didn't Mind, the Results Didn't Matter

Rugby can expand to fill the time available. If needed, it can be stretched out to take up most of the weekend.

To start with, it's not just the professionals who need to navigate their way through a series of pre-match rituals and superstitions. Even bungling amateurs need to spend a little time preparing and orientating themselves before a match. Getting a body like mine fully ready to withstand the stress and strain of a weekly game of rugby takes considerable planning and preparation.

My body is a temple of course, but sadly one in which I worship cake, chips and real ale. It took a little while to realise that, although a large round belly was not necessarily an impediment to playing, it helped if it wasn't full of food too close to the kick-off. Every Saturday morning I needed to organise enough calories to work their way through my system in time to be on hand and available to the bits of me that were going to have to work. I needed an empty stomach during the match but not one that was starving hungry either. It was a delicate balance and it took great care to get it right.

A large, well-timed plate of scrambled eggs, and a possible side order of bacon, on wholegrain toast was my Saturday breakfast of choice and I convinced myself and family that spending the rest of the morning drinking coffee and reading the paper was an essential part of the preparation that would ensure a good performance and guarantee an injury-free game. In the days before I could afford a satnav, I would print off detailed directions to the pitch if we were playing away, and I might even organise a few copies for other drivers. At around 11 a.m. I would neatly fold my kit and place it all in the reverse order of need in my kitbag. I was then free to make the last-minute calls to sort out changes of playing personnel and opposition.

About an hour before the game, or longer if we were playing away from home, players would gather in the bar of the clubhouse. Handshakes and a little gentle banter were followed by more phone calls to chase up the tardy and recruit friends of friends to fill any gaps on the team sheet. Then it was either into the cars or into the changing rooms.

Once in the changing rooms there was the ritual scrounging of the tape. Many players seem to like to use strips of electrical tape to hold their socks up and possibly also to keep their boot laces done up. This has never been a problem for me as I have little fat legs which, once they have been squeezed into a pair of rugby socks, exert sufficient outward pressure to counter the sock-dropping forces of gravity. However, anorexic backs preparing for an afternoon standing around in the cold need to ensure that as much of their body stays covered for as long as possible. Normally only one person had actually remembered to bring any tape, typically someone whose day job was either physiotherapist or electrician. They would then moan and complain as a succession of poverty-pleading teenagers worked through the roll, strapping the tape around their calves.

In dribs and very reluctant drabs the players would amble out onto the pitch. Backs normally went first as they liked to have a little runaround and practise kicking the ball to each other. Forwards tended to save their energy and wander out a little later, with the front row typically last of all. By the time I made it out to the pitch, there would normally be a little game of touch rugby going on, with two sides lined up playing across the pitch. This was often the only time during the course of the afternoon when I would actually receive a pass and make one.

For one friend of mine called Barry, the pre-match touch game was all he ever saw of the match. I had been pestering him to play for months but as he lived miles away in the Norfolk countryside it was a massive effort for him to get to a game. Nevertheless, he was fit and keen and made the three-hour journey from his rural barn he was converting to be with us. He was clearly looking forward to the game, fired up and excited, telling me with great enthusiasm how much running and training he had been doing over the previous months. As the pace of the pre-match touch game picked up, Barry was keen to show how 'in shape' he was, in order to secure a place in the starting line-up. His side had the ball and was attacking as he sprinted towards a gap calling for the pass. As he caught the ball he suddenly started hopping about, wincing in pain, having pulled a muscle in his leg. He spent the rest of the game grumpily hobbling along the touchline before embarking on the long journey home.

At some point the game of touch was called to an end and then there was a vague attempt to stretch off any muscles. Thinking about it now, perhaps Barry might have got more of a game if we did these things in a different order. Anyway, I would attempt to get everyone together into a little cluster and lead them off jogging around the pitch and making them go through a sequence of high knee steps, heel flicks, lunges and sideways running steps. We would stand in a circle and I would suggest some half-remembered upper body stretches. I would then try and remember everyone's name and what position they were playing, and run through the starting line-up.

Backs and forwards would split up with the backs running off to practise sprinting around the pitch and throwing great long passes to each other. The forwards would meanwhile stand around for a bit trying to remember the line-out calls. The two halves of the team would then reunite and attempt to run through a sequence or two of unopposed play.

By this point I would be exhausted and in no fit state to play a game of rugby. There would be a brief huddle, in which I would desperately wrack my brain for some piece of strategic, tactical or motivational information, and we would line up for the referee's starting whistle.

No national anthems or haka for us in the lowly Surrey leagues. It was straight on with the game. I did, however, hear of one touring side, made up of occasional players and the odd Oxbridge Blue, who decided to introduce a haka for every game in their tour of Italy. The New Zealand pre-match war dance involves Maori chants about hairy men and the rising sun and is accompanied by exaggerated hand gestures, wide staring eyes and jumping in the air, in an attempt to intimidate the opposition. The English tourists couldn't quite manage to learn any Maori so opted instead to use a popular nursery rhyme, Humpty Dumpty, shouted to the same rhythm and movements used by the All Blacks. Try it and see. It kind of works: 'Hump-er-ty Dump-er-ty sat on a wall. Hump-er-ty Dump-er-ty had a great fall etc.' The Italian teams they were playing against apparently were not able to translate quickly enough to realise what was going on, and so stood, respectfully observing the ritual before every match.

After the game there were beers to be drunk, hangovers to be slept through, match reports to be written and muscle strains to be eased away over several hours in a Radox-filled bath. Before you knew it, the next selection committee meeting was looming and the whole cycle began again. Part of the post-match ritual in my second season in charge of the Warlingham 4th XV was coming up with a decent excuse for our inevitable defeats. I wasn't getting much better at leading a side to victory, but I was getting much better at spinning the results, highlighting injustices and clutching at straws.

The statistics, however, were not looking good. As the year drew to its conclusion we were still bumping along the bottom of the bottom league in Surrey. Our defeats had been perhaps a little more heroic but they were still defeats. We managed to snatch defeat from the jaws of victory, scoring seven tries against Merton at home, only to lose in the final moments of the game to a cheeky drop goal from in front of our posts.

'How do you score seven tries at home and lose?' asked Smudger in the bar that evening. It was a fair question and one for which I did not have a real answer. In the close games little things can make all the difference and as one of the littlest things on the pitch, I needed to take my share of responsibility.

We were utterly frustrated to lose away to Old Rutlishians, particularly as they had failed to organise three people capable of playing in the front row. As a result, all the scrums had to be 'uncontested', which means that no one is allowed to push and whichever side puts the ball in has to be allowed to win it. This is always deeply irritating, particularly for forwards like me and the rest of my ageing pack. The thing we like about rugby is all the pushing and shoving in the scrum. It is probably the most fun you can have with your clothes on and the most exercise you can have without having to run around like an idiot.

The risk of an inexperienced front row doing themselves a mischief isn't very high, but if something did go wrong and a scrum collapsed awkwardly, the kind of injury one might get would be fairly serious. No one really wants to spend the rest of their life in a wheelchair, or worse, for the sake of an overenthusiastic group hug. Uncontested scrums are a sensible way to make sure that something close to a game of rugby still goes ahead but they do take the heart out of the game. Old Ruts had made a bit of a habit of under-resourcing their pack. As a result, my props were severely underemployed. These are gentlemen who live for the test of strength in the scrum. Without a decent front-row battle they were left looking for something else to burn off the calories. Fortunately Old Ruts had a deeply irritating, floppy-haired captain with a tediously whiney voice. Generally terrorising him and giving him something to whine about gave my frustrated props something else to do throughout the match.

We had also lost away at Streatham in spite of me making my annual tackle in the game. I was normally way too slow and scared to get involved in stopping an opposition player but on this occasion I just had to brace myself as he ran towards me. More by luck than judgement, my shoulder lined up with the softer bits of his anatomy and I managed to get enough of my arms round him to make him stop. Either that, or he just needed a rest after running around all afternoon. Arnie, their well-insulated and deceptively fast back, humiliated us again, as he had in my first fixture as captain.

I should have realised that the Streatham game wasn't going to go well, when before the kick-off their hooker, who I recognised from previous fixtures, introduced himself as the referee. He was the smallest person on their side and owned up straight away that he had never officiated before and wasn't entirely sure which end of the whistle to blow in. Still, we went ahead with their little hooker running along beside us more like an overenthusiastic spectator than a match official. We heard very little from him and instead the game became largely self-regulating. Afterwards the referee admitted that most of the time he had forgotten what he was supposed to be doing and when he did see an infringement of the rules, he had been waiting for someone else to blow the whistle and call proceedings to a halt.

Somehow we managed to keep up morale, by collecting injustices and congratulating ourselves on managing to field a team at all. Random fat blokes were still getting some exercise and a break from the routine every week. Still, the results should have been getting better. I was getting decent-enough players but perhaps that vital element of leadership and motivation was missing. This captaincy malarkey was more complicated than I had first thought. I have a degree in psychology from Oxford for goodness' sake. I ought to be able to find something that would make the team click but nothing I could dredge up from those ivory tower days was of any use. I needed something more to help get my team into the right space mentally to secure a much-needed win.

The opportunity came with our last game of the season to try something a little different, improve our mental toughness, whatever that might mean, and carve out a decent result to finish off the year.

Our 1st team had travelled away to Eltham. The 2nd's and 3rd's games were cancelled. It fell to the 4ths to provide the entertainment for the two or three men and a dog that had failed to travel with the 1st team and had wandered up to the clubhouse in search of a pint and a game to watch.

It is always delightful when a few people turn up to watch you play. No one has to pay for a ticket to enjoy the game as a spectator at this sort of level but they will probably spend a little money behind the bar. Their presence helps to keep your spirits up when you are at the wrong end of a massacre. Even better, they can witness and join in the celebrations when things go well. When a tree falls over in a forest and no one is there to listen, you can never be entirely sure whether it has made a noise. Similarly, when a fat bloke falls over with the ball at the end of a muddy field, if there are no spectators can you ever be entirely certain whether he has scored a try?

As we were the only home side, the 1st-team changing rooms were empty. Normally the 4th XV would have to change in a corner of a large, cold and grubby communal changing area squeezed in between one or two other sides. Opposing players would regularly wander through in search of their own room, the showers or the loos and so there was no real opportunity to talk tactics, strategy or do any sort of bonding, shouting or communal snorting of Deep Heat fumes.

I saw a chance to give the 4ths a badly needed psychological boost and went in search of the 1st-team changing room key. I tracked down the club duty member for the day who was in charge of organising putting out the pitch flags, pumping up the match balls and filling the communal post-match bath. I pulled rank as best I could and extracted the 1st-team keys from him. With a little flourish, I led my men into the private and palatial 1st-team changing room in the hope that some cognitive reprogramming, a winning mentality or maybe just inhaling some of the residual testosterone in the air would give us the playing edge we needed. Sadly, all we found were a couple of jars of extra-strong hair gel and a faint whiff of Lynx Tropical man spray. It was going to take more than this.

I decided that we would also play our match on the hallowed turf of the 1st-team pitch and persuaded the duty member to put out the flags and post protectors accordingly. This pristine and lovingly tonsured pitch would make a nice change from the smaller, undulating, distant corner of the playing fields we were normally allocated. Perhaps this would help raise our game. If not, at least our supporters wouldn't need to walk that far from the bar and they would have some nice wooden railing and advertising hoardings to lean on.

I had flicked through a few sports psychology books and some had talked about the importance of visualisation. If we could visualise ourselves playing like a winning side then apparently we would play like one. I wasn't going to be able to persuade my rabble into anything as weird and woolly as that but I did manage to get the side running through a pre-match warm-up more along the lines of the routine used by the 1st team. We replaced our typical, casual pre-match rituals with tightly drilled groups of four players at a time, simultaneously stepping through a series of increasingly complicated dynamic stretches. Muscles we didn't know we had were loosened and minds were focused.

Cranleigh had brought with them a rather large front row and as a result they had our pack going backwards most of the afternoon. One by one my props and their replacements were broken and hobbled off to the touchline. Eventually I had to move one place to the right in the scrum and try and prop for the first time ever to keep the scrums contested.

Tom Osbourne at scrum half had an increasingly difficult afternoon, attempting to extract the ball from a retreating and crumbling scrum. His passing, which was never brilliant at the best of times, became more and more frantic and random as he tried desperately to get us out of trouble. By the time the ball bobbled and bounced its way to Ben Hathaway playing at number 10, or descended from the near-earth-orbit that Tom had sent it into, Ben was surrounded by opposing players and generally torn limb from limb. The rest of our backs watched on helplessly, waiting in vain for a ball that would never reach them. Meanwhile Cranleigh ran in a succession of simple tries.

Things needed to improve and in the second half, from somewhere, we gained a little pride and a little bit more oomph. Perhaps it was the responsibility of playing on the 1st-team pitch. Perhaps it was the fact that it was the last game of the season and there was no point holding anything back. Perhaps with the regular playing all season we were actually a little bit fitter than we thought. Who knows? But from somewhere deep inside us a residual ounce or two of self-respect kicked in and we began a bit of a fightback.

After a little burst of forwards pressure I found myself following up a kick from Ben Hathaway and leading the charge towards the Cranleigh full back who was shaping to kick the ball back to us.

Angry and determined, I puffed myself up and tried to fill up as much of his field of vision as possible as I ran towards the kicker. To my surprise the ball flew straight at me and bounced off my arms and bobbled along the floor.

Had I been the finished rugby-playing article, I would at this point have bent down, scooped up the ball with one hand and carried it the short distance to the try line. Sadly, the combination of a vast belly and vertebrae that had been having a difficult afternoon in the scrum meant that I couldn't really bend down terribly well. However, it wasn't going to be necessary. Flying in behind me was Dave Millard, whose wealth as a self-employed property developer means that he really doesn't need to work very much and instead spends most of his time in the gym, stretching and flexing his body for exactly this sort of eventuality. Dave did the honours, picked up the ball and shot over the try line to finally get us some points onto the 1st-team scoreboard.

We kept up the pressure and slowed down the rate at which Cranleigh were scoring. We weren't going to win but we did manage to restore a little pride and put on a bit more of a show for the supporters. As we approached the final whistle, we were desperately defending deep in our own half. Somehow Tom managed to get the ball to Ben with enough time for him to kick it away before being flattened once again. A massive kick got us out of trouble but also opened up another opportunity. Our winger Shane Smith had been seriously underemployed all afternoon and had some surplus energy reserves left. A part-time carpet fitter, Shane is also a graduate of the famous performing arts school in Croydon that has given the world the singers Adele and Jessie J. He was making a bit of a name for himself, so he told us, on the

Malia/Ayia Napa club circuit, under the name of DJ Reckless. Sensing an opportunity and still full of running, he set off at a blistering pace and managed to grab the ball. With the rest of the side willing him on, he ran half the length of the pitch using his best dance floor moves to weave in and out of defenders. I shouted, 'Go on, Shane. All the way, son.' And with a final burst of speed he made it over the try line and planted the ball firmly on the ground. A conversion followed and the referee blew the final whistle. Our season had ended with the perfect final flourish.

We were still roughly the third-worst side in Surrey, but we were putting up a decent fight and enjoying the game week in week out. Our collection of carpet fitters come club DJs, property developers, floppy-haired city bankers and trainee Methodist ministers were still together putting up a decent fight, continuing to accommodate each other's weaknesses and playing to our modest and occasional strengths.

Still, I felt I could give the side a little more. I was tiring slightly of the hapless performances we were turning in. Perhaps I could take it all just a little more seriously? Maybe with some remedial coaching and a less haphazard approach to team selection, I could drag the side off the bottom of the league for my last season as captain before identifying a successor and handing over the reins. I realised that I couldn't do this on my own and so, over the summer, I set about looking for people who could help.

Chapter 17

The Skivington Waltz

Some people have said that the only real problem with English rugby is the length of the English summer. The English summer might be short but for a rugby fanatic it is far too long. During the warmer months of the year, the lack of a game every weekend, and all the rest that went with it, created a huge void in my life, as it does for every rugby player. Whilst there were plans and preparations to make for the next season, there was a definite vacancy for an activity to keep my now finely honed body occupied and at the peak of physical fitness. Perhaps that is a bit of an exaggeration. I wasn't exactly physically fit but I had dragged my metabolism off the floor and my body mass index was down to slightly lower than a sack of lard.

There were a few candidates for summer alternatives to rugby. Touch rugby can in theory be played all year round. It doesn't involve tackling and so the hard ground is less of a problem. However, without the rucks and mauls that normally come after a tackle, the game can get a little repetitive. There isn't really enough variety in the game for those of us with a short attention span and a low boredom threshold. Alternatively, rugby pitches lend themselves well to a game that has decided to brand itself 'Ultimate Frisbee'. A good few summer evenings at Warlingham were agreeably passed flinging a frisbee around and playing to a set of rules a little like a non-contact version of American Football. After an awful lot of running around, passing and blocking, the aim of the game was to catch the frisbee in the end zone. Sadly, my frisbee-handling skills were not much better than my rugby ball-handling skills and, in painful reliving of my primary school playground days, I was invariably the last to be picked for a side.

A strange hybrid called Net Rugby is played every year on Clapham Common, organised by a couple of Warlingham club members. A couple of the massive wooden net structures were brought along to our playing fields and so I decided to have a go that summer. In this game two teams competed to try and get a rugby ball into huge nets at either end of the pitch. The ball could be passed forwards as well as back and again there seemed to be quite a lot more running around involved. Quite why this was seen as a summer sport remained a mystery to me. It still involved full-contact tackling and, as a result, a lot of grazed skin shredded up by the hard ground.

Far and away the best summer diversion at Warlingham was when we teamed up with the netball club that shares the facilities, for their summer party and AGM tournament. As 4th-team captain I was invited to lead a mixed netball side, with boys from the 4ths and girls from their youth team. The Inbetweeners were particularly excited as they would get to run around with some members of the opposite sex. Some of the older club members also got a little excited too, but for different reasons. The opportunity to dress up in netball skirts and bibs seemed too good to be missed. Plenty of macho bravado was in evidence as the chaps wondered how hard this girls' game could possibly be.

It turned out to be a lot harder than it looked.

As I gently made my way around the court, I was harassed, hassled and blocked relentlessly by the teenage daughter of one of the rugby club coaches. Young Miss Sheridan seemed to be wherever I looked and in my way whatever I tried to do. For a non-contact sport there was an awful lot of barging and elbowing going on as I struggled to get hold of the ball and pass it. I was harried whenever I got the ball and had to twist and turn to try and get a clear opportunity to pass. No wonder girls drop out of sports if this is the main thing on offer to them at school as teenagers. This was exhausting and maddeningly frustrating. The experienced girls of course ran rings around us and left the boys bewildered and confused. With Miss Sheridan proving to be an omnipresent obstacle, I had to resort to moving in very unfamiliar directions and using bits of me that had long since gone into retirement. Inevitably a muscle I didn't know I had, and had never previously needed, pinged and I hobbled off humiliated.

It then turned out that the real reason the event had been organised was that the girls wanted to use the boys' communal bath. With swimming costumes and bubbles to protect everyone's virtue and modesty, some of the girls and a few of the braver boys and the pervier older men piled into the bath for a post-tournament celebration. For me that was a far more terrifying sight than when the bath was full of muddy, sweaty and mangled rugby players and so, with my legs no longer functioning properly, I took refuge in a corner of the bar until things had calmed down.

Apart from this annual cross-dressing and communal bathing encounter with the netball girls, the rugby club is a predominantly male preserve. There are a few wives, mums, girlfriends and their mates to be found on the touchline and around the bar but it mostly remains a sanctuary for chaps and that I'm sure has its good and bad sides. The all-male environment does give us guys a chance to relax a little. With our limited powers of communication it is sometimes a struggle to interact with women without tripping over one of the million different ways we can offend and upset them without ever understanding fully what we have done wrong. A little time spent with the simpler sex is a nice way to unwind before braving the complexity of mixed gender interaction and unscrambling the unfathomable codes of female communication.

The club is not an entirely male preserve, however, and had benefited from the services of female physios for several seasons, under the guidance of Pete 'Magic Hands' Mattison. Very occasionally when the 2nd and 3rd teams had been without a fixture, the 4ths were blessed with a fit young tracksuited physiotherapist on the touchline poised with a medical bag full of sprays, strapping and freezer packs ready to come on and tend to any injuries. At my uglier and more remedial end of the club, players were far less used to receiving the care and ministrations of attractive and attentive young women. As a result the numbers of injuries and strains received seemed to massively increase and I would struggle to keep fifteen players on the pitch. For some reason, when the only thing to look forward to on the touchline was John Glover with a bucket of cold water and a grubby sponge, nobody seemed to get injured.

The all-male atmosphere becomes a little sterile after a while, it must be said. After a few hours in the clubhouse following a game, the younger players will head off to Croydon nightclubs and bars for a more balanced social scene and the older ones will head home to their wives and families. The healthier rugby clubs around the country have women's sides playing every week and my club is probably weaker without one. I hope eventually someone will organise a women's team and I suspect the clubhouse will stay fuller for longer in the evenings as a result.

I've not played a mixed game of rugby myself but I have heard of one game played by a friend of mine when she was a student. This was an end-of-term game played for a bit of fun between the men's and women's sides of the college. At half-time, the women were several points behind. So instead of passing round the orange segments, they passed round a tube of Deep Heat and made sure they each had a good couple of handfuls. As the game started again, they took every possible opportunity to get their hands into the boys' nether regions. Under different circumstances the girls' wandering hands might have been more than welcome. However, soon most of the men were significantly impeded, hobbling around clutching at their shorts as the active ingredients took their rather undesired effect.

After a summer of diverting distractions it became time to start once again putting in an appearance at the rugby club on training nights and girding my netball-strained loins. As the start of the new season approached I began to gear up for the contest ahead and prepare a strategy for doing perhaps that little bit better than last year. It was not quite enough to just turn up. We had achieved Woody Allen's eighty per cent of success by doing that. I wanted to work on the other twenty per cent.

My criteria for success in rugby had initially been fairly low. The fact that I was playing rugby at all in what was becoming my forties was pretty impressive. Having studiously avoided any physical activity for most of my life, this was a minor miracle. More than a fad or a phase it was a genuine lifestyle change. After decades of sloth, I had become the sort of person who plays a sport regularly every week. Who would have thought it?

I had also become someone who could get a team together, almost at the drop of a hat. I had a phone book full of enough potential players of a sufficiently wide range of shapes and sizes that with one group text message I could get more or less fifteen of them into a rugby club changing room somewhere in Surrey, prepared to subject themselves to eighty minutes of pretty intense physical activity under my command. The next step was to develop something approaching a set of leadership skills and to start to use them.

Leaders, according to the sports psychology manuals, need to set goals and so, at the beginning of my third and final season, I decided to set some: the first was to drag the team off the bottom of the league, and the second more important one was to identify a new captain and hand the side on. In the corporate world it's called succession planning. I wanted to see if I could recruit and induce someone who would be able to keep the 4th XV going and lead it to new heights or, to be honest, a first ever height. We had created something out of almost nothing and I didn't want the 4ths to go back to that.

Dragging the side off the bottom of the league was going to be a bit more of a challenge. The bearded and beer-stained gentlemen of the Surrey RFC committee had decided, in their infinite wisdom, to merge the two bottom leagues and create one new super league, or more accurately one new not-so-super-league, called the 'Foundation' League. The league name was no doubt chosen by the committee to motivate and inspire us but instead for me it conjured up images of being little better than a heap of builders' rubble to be buried underground to prop up the multi-storey edifice of Surrey rugby.

We were scheduled to play each side only once in the season rather than the usual routine of playing opposition sides at home and away. On our current form we would end up at the bottom of a much larger league, losing by much larger margins to sides who had previously played in the league above us. Instead of being worse than six out of the eight other members of our league, we would be much worse than fifteen of the seventeen other members of our league and would thus get unceremoniously spanked slightly more often.

So things had to change. Losing every week would become depressing and I would struggle to hold onto players if I was not careful. No one wants to be humiliated every weekend and we would surely lose out to the competing Croydon attractions of burning down furniture shops or joyriding in Thornton Heath. We needed to improve our fitness and technical ability if we were to stand a chance and so I dragged myself and a few other players up to the pre-season training sessions.

There was a little bit of a buzz around the club at the start of the season. There had been a surge of new players; young fit types, fresh from some good rugby-playing local schools. They were unlikely to play for me in the lowly 4ths but they might make selection committees easier with perhaps some of the older players drifting down to the bottom sides.

Guest coaches were being brought in to introduce some new specialist strategies for different aspects of the game. One of these was a complex new line-out calls system, which everyone was struggling to comprehend.

What normally happens in a line-out at the lower levels of the game is that ten or fifteen minutes before the kick-off, the forwards waddle off to one corner of the pitch to try out a few throw-ins. The two heaviest players get hold of the lightest and lift him up by his knees, thighs or shorts and the hooker practises throwing the ball at him. The idea is that if your jumper can jump higher than the other team's, and you can time and target your throw to meet your catcher's hands at their highest point, you will mostly win your own throw-ins.

In the unlikely event that you can perfect a simple throw and have it caught reliably and there are still a few minutes to spare, then conversation amongst the forwards will turn to options and line-out calls. If one or two more players can be found prepared to do some lifting and another can be found who is light enough to be lifted then your team has the option of two different targets to throw the ball to. If that is one more than the opposing side then again you will have an advantage. You then need a system of calls to let your side know which person to throw up into the air without letting the opposition know.

The system of calls needs to be very simple indeed. These are forwards we are talking about, not known for their intellectual prowess. At Warlingham, three words would be chosen, for example 'Thames', 'Rowing' and 'Club'. If the call began with a letter from the first word, e.g. Tiramisu, Horatio, Avocado or Manchester etc, then the ball would be thrown to the front of the line-out for the person being lifted there to catch the ball. If the call began with a letter from the second word, e.g. Rabbit, Orinoco, Westminster etc, then the ball would be thrown slightly further to the middle of the line-out for the person standing fourth or fifth in the line to catch. The third word would be only used in the unlikely event that the hooker was capable of throwing the ball any further and reaching the end of the line-out.

I have only managed a long throw once in all my time playing rugby. I had my little brother playing with me and he was lurking at the end of the line-out towards the end of a long gruelling game. Nathan is reasonably fit whereas the rest of the forwards on both sides were completely knackered. With a couple of knowing glances Nathan and I twigged that a long throw might be on, but mostly because no one else would have the energy to compete for the ball. Without bothering with a line-out call to let anyone else know what we were doing, I arched my full 5 foot 6 inch frame back as far as it would go, with my belly pushed forwards like a pregnant woman trying to get a seat on a train, and then threw the ball as far as I could. Unusually it travelled more or less in a straight line in between the two packs who were still mostly catching their breath and waiting for the call. My talented little brother caught it and shot off to score a try.

Normally, for line-out codes to work all the forwards need to be able to spell and remember the code and the hooker must be able to think up new words for each call in order to keep the opposition guessing. Calls like Psychology, Knife and Pneumatic are for obvious reasons best avoided. For some reason also the word 'Eight' seems to confuse props who can't get their head round the idea that a number can start with a letter. At this stage, most forwards will have reached the limit of their processing powers. If they haven't warmed up properly one or two may have pulled a muscle in their brain. All of them will want to have a little lie down to recover from the mental exertions of learning the code before the game actually starts.

It had taken me a few seasons to get my head around the basics of the line-out and to be able to throw the ball consistently and accurately at the person who was jumping for it. So the prospect of a new system filled me with dread. The new system was known as

'Skivington' after George Skivington, the Wasps lock who had used it or something like it with some success. It involved a complicated choreography with forwards swapping positions in the line-out and a decision taken at the last possible moment about who to throw the ball to, depending on how the defending opposition had reacted to the various decoy moves. It was desperately confusing but when it worked it was beautiful, a work of art. The Bolshoi Ballet have nothing with the same level of elegance and poetry as a perfectly executed Skivington line-out move.

The 1st-team forwards had nailed the Skivington and were kind enough to demonstrate how it worked to the few 3rd- and 4th-team players who had made it up to training. Slowly we got our respective heads around it. It was hard work and even involved one player spending an entire day at work designing an animated PowerPoint presentation to try and make it clearer. As we warmed up for our first 4th-XV game of the new season, I was keen to see if we could use it to raise the standard of the game in the new Surrey Foundation League.

Somehow I had managed to get thirty-one names onto the team sheet for our opening fixture against Croydon. For our last two journeys to our near neighbours' ground I had barely managed to get my team numbers into double figures. Even after the usual process of rugby osmosis, by which players drift off towards the captain most likely to give them a decent game, I still managed to have twenty-seven players. As it was a pre-season friendly and Croydon had no other home games, we were spared the usual molehill steeplechase and moved onto their more pristine, if a little sandy, 1st-team pitch.

Playing on the 1st-team pitch meant that Croydon might have been employing a few 1st-team ringers. Or at the very least, the psychological boost of playing on the big boys' field was more powerful at this end of Surrey. The downside of having so many available players was that I had to keep chopping and changing people around, bringing people on and off to make sure everyone got something of a game. As a result we were a bit muddled and confused. This was of course not helped by trying to explain the new Skivington line-out system to the vast majority of the forwards who would rather have a bikini wax performed on them by a Bolivian shot-putter than attend a training session voluntarily.

Croydon had a smaller number of players, most of whom had played the previous week, so they were a little less rusty and better organised. They were scoring tries rather more efficiently than we were and the Skivington system was leaving our forwards standing around scratching their heads in confusion after every failed line-out throw-in.

We were struggling somewhat but not as much as the referee. As camp as Christmas and terribly frail, our allocated match official had only very recently been handed his ceremonial whistle, notepad and pencil after graduating from referee school. He sort of minced around the pitch, tentatively calling a halt to proceedings only very rarely when he felt brave enough to blow his whistle. This was turned to our advantage at one point when there was a very obvious knock-on caused by one of our players.

A 'knock-on' is caused when someone fumbles a catch and the ball bounces off them going illegally forward. It should result in a scrum, with the other side getting the advantage of putting the ball in. This particular offence was so obvious that everyone near the ball stopped playing and began to think about forming up for the scrum. Our referee, however, was still very reluctant to blow his whistle, perhaps concerned that pursing his lips too often might give him unsightly wrinkles. John Waghorn knew the important maxim 'Play to the Whistle.' If the whistle hadn't been blown, then officially no offence had been committed and play could continue. John grabbed the ball and set off on a run down the pitch.

John is a good friend and a fellow member of the front-row fraternity. A driving instructor by day, he is more used to a sedentary lifestyle, and achieving any sort of speed without the aid of an internal combustion engine was always going to be troublesome. In his fitter days he has held his own with a place in the 1st team, but the joys of a pint or three, some chips and/or possibly a curry has lent him a certain degree of cuddliness.

John's quick thinking nonetheless gave him a clear head start on the opposition. He soon found himself with a free run at lots of space and took the ball well down the pitch. We could see he was tiring a little as the long barbeque summer was weighing a little on his waistline. Looking around he quickly found someone to pass to, having spotted his old school friend Matt White. Matt had missed the end of the previous season with a dose of something unpleasant and medical, but had clearly come back refreshed and rejuvenated. He shot off to the end of the pitch to collect his first try for the club. He might have scored another one later had it not been for the fact that with the excitement of crossing the line for a second time he lost control of the ball. From where I was catching my breath, it looked like the ball had mysteriously turned into a giant bar of soap, slipping out of Matt's grasp at the crucial moment.

Meanwhile, for the Inbetweeners, a hot summer clubbing and posing in Ayia Napa or Ibiza had honed their teenage bodies and they were beginning to grow into their skin. The little boy-mountain Kieran had discovered he could now run at grown men and knock them over pretty much at will and he was clearly enjoying it. Another, called Rory, hadn't quite worked out how to speak to adults or arrive anywhere on time, but put him in a number 9 shirt and position him just behind a scrum and suddenly he was in total command of the game, organising attack after attack and terrorising the opposition. They were turning out to be quite useful.

For a first game of the season I felt reasonably fit and a bit more confident handling the ball. My summer spent running around with a frisbee and trying various versions of netball hadn't been a complete waste of time. The Inbetweeners had also benefited from a distracting summer involving, I suspected, plenty of sun, sex and sangria. We had put on a good display for what was only a friendly and the omens were looking very good.

Chapter 18

What's in a Nickname?

By hanging on as 4th-team captain for a third season, I was now the most experienced player of 'Captain's Poker'. I was also getting a little more ruthless about hanging onto and looking after my better rugby players. Whilst I wasn't going to repeal the 4th-team motto that 'No one gives anyone any sh*t for being sh*t', I was planning to try and encourage a few players that were a bit less sh*t to turn out and play for me more regularly.

This year there had been a rule change that meant there was more pressure to have lots of front-row players. Any side that ran out of props in a game and had to go to uncontested scrums was going to be forced to play with only fourteen men. This was in order to stop quick sides with a weaker pack from pretending to have broken a prop and then running around and scoring lots of tries.

So when a prop dropped out of the 1st team late on a Friday night, there was a knock-on effect throughout the club. They would raid the 2nd team, promoting someone who was only too happy to pull on a 1st-team shirt. His captain would then sniff around the 3rd-team front row – not a pleasant image, I'm sorry, but you know what I mean. Then, when the 3rd-team captain and I had our Saturday morning conversation, it went something like this.

3rd-team captain: 'Hey, Gaugey.'

Most people in the club are known by a corruption of their surname. This is the simplest version, formed by simply adding a 'y' onto the end of the name, normally only used with single-syllable surnames. The 3rd-team captain, Chris Redman, was allocated the slightly more complex construction of removing the last syllable, replacing it with 'ers', and doubling the middle consonant.

Me: 'Hey, Redders. How are you doing for numbers?'

This opening gambit is crucial. Note how I have carefully avoided revealing my own hand at this stage. When selection is difficult and player numbers are low, there is always a possibility that one captain will give up the ghost and cry off his game. One whiff of a dwindling side and the other captains will circle around like vultures looking to pick a few juicy players out of the carcass of the disintegrating team.

Redders: 'Not good. The twos have taken my prop so I'm struggling for a front row. I'm having to bring Chappers (Chris

Chapman – see surname corruption rule 2) or Spike (a completely made-up name, possibly based on a misjudged haircut) up from the back row and I may have to hook. You?'

Me: 'I've got just about fifteen players.'

This is meaningless, as I've always got just about fifteen players – regardless of how many players I actually have and no matter whom I'm talking to. That way other captains don't try and persuade me to cry off the game so they can hoover up my players. Also, other players are more likely to turn up if they think I've got enough players to start but potentially a shortage in one or two positions so that they might get a bit of a game.

I continue, 'I'm looking for a prop too.'

Risky move this, as it implies that I therefore have at least one prop who could be fair game if Redders decides to pull rank and claim him. Quick rethink.

'I've got Matt Buckland,' (newish recruit – surname corruption pending) 'who's really a winger.'

Actually he looks nothing like a winger and I've never seen him catch the ball or run but it's enough to put Redders off.

'And then I'll probably have to prop, which I can't really do.'

Obviously he can't promote me to the 3rds as I'm the captain of the 4ths and am really too small and pathetic to be in his huge pack of forwards.

Redders: 'I might try and get Bazzer… ' (Barry Ruddock – who seems to have been assigned the football-like corruption of his first name to avoid the nautical-sounding option of 'Rudders') ' … to step up, failing that we'll have to go uncontested.'

Yes! Result! He blinked first, conceding the possibility of going uncontested rather than taking any of my players. My apology for a front row remains intact.

Me: 'Oh well, good luck – see you in the bar afterwards.'

Redders: 'And you – see you there.'

This is Redders' first season as a captain. He'll learn.

When I make it onto the pitch that Saturday, it turns out that one of my new players can also prop. Naturally I am careful not to tell anyone else that, and avoid mentioning it in the match report.

Over the course of the previous season around seventy different players had turned out and pulled on a 4th-team shirt. Many had only played one or two games before thinking better of it. Each week there was a little time spent by the team learning new names and shuffling around positions. If we were going to win a little more often than we lost we would need a slightly more settled squad.

To generate regular players you need regular games so, working with the club administrator, I started to try and fill more of the gaps in between league fixtures with friendly games. If our league opposition couldn't rustle up a side to honour a fixture we would ring around and try to get another team to play in order to keep our hand in and maintain the team momentum.

With my more assertive approach to selection, we started to turn up to games with sufficient men and occasionally we were even on time. For our first league game we were away to Streatham and

Croydon and, in spite of having to negotiate our way through the Saturday afternoon shopping traffic to get to their ground in Thornton Heath, we were there with plenty of players and in plenty of time. Streatham and Croydon were still running around looking for a couple of props whilst we were running through a disciplined set of pre-match drills.

The only slight problem was that we had failed to bring any rugby balls with us for the pre-match warm-up. When I say 'we' I suppose I really mean 'I' had forgotten to bring any balls, but this lapse in organisation was to be no impediment to the newly resourceful and committed 4th team. Rummaging around the Streatham playing fields one of the boys found a discarded football, one of the round ones. It may have been the wrong shape but we made the best of it, using it for our warm-up drills whilst we waited for the Streatham team to get its own act together.

Something had definitely changed in our mindset. Normally the 4th XV on a visit to Streatham could expect to be humiliated at the hands and legs of Arnie, their oversized and turbocharged back. This time our beanpole-like video editor Mark Bright, aka Brighty, put in an early crunching tackle that had him hobbling around for the rest of the game. OK, so he might have hobbled over our try line once or twice but we had made the point that we weren't going to be totally intimidated just because we weren't playing at home. Eager to join in the fun, property magnate Dave Millard finished him off with another big hit towards the end of the second half.

Tackling became our new hobby and all over the pitch, previously shy and retiring players dropped their shoulders and thumped them into the midriff of any Streatham player unlucky enough to get the ball. We were tackling at will and as a result were able to steal the ball occasionally and score some points.

Over the summer Streatham had acquired some new young players who, although inexperienced, were massive. Fast food joints in the local area must be the place to invest because some of these kids had packed in more calories in a few short years than would reasonably feed a small Third World country. However, our new tackling demons were not to be deterred. Rather than backing off and letting these south London leviathans amble through our defences as normal, we started tackling in pairs. Danny Gillespie, a newish refugee from the association game, and Matt Buckland, our strange winger/prop hybrid, joined forces to stop a rampaging Streatham giant, who had just steamrollered through the rest of our team. Danny and Matt, perhaps frustrated by their shared lack of a decent nickname between them, sought to prove themselves by each of them grabbing hold of separate bits of the vast attacker somewhere just below his centre of gravity. With a thud, the Streatham player hit the ground but an additional ear-splitting crack could also be heard all across the pitch. As Danny and Matt disentangled themselves, the Streatham player was left with his foot pointing towards the back of his knee. Inbetweener Kieran, who had just arrived, hoping to pick up the ball and run off and score, took one look and, with his most impressive display of speed all season, ran to the opposite end of the pitch to get reacquainted with his breakfast instead.

It was all a bit of a shock. We didn't know our own strength. Danny and Matt began to look a little queasy as we waited for an ambulance. The young lad was whisked off to Mayday Hospital in Croydon and we reluctantly restarted the game and went through the motions until the final whistle. There was something new and a little bit scary in the 4th XV this year. Somehow we were going to have to channel it into winning points rather than breaking ankles. The artists formerly known as the Third-Worst Side in Surrey were rebranding themselves into The Mighty 4s.

Chapter 19

No Sport for Old Men

As part of the campaign to drag my beloved 4th XV off the bottom of the Surrey Foundation League, we had enlisted the services of a dedicated 3rd- and 4th-team coach called Phil for training on a Tuesday and Thursday night. Armed with a ring binder and some photocopied notes, Phil took us off to a separate corner of the training pitch, a safe distance away from the drooling and dangerous 1st-team monsters, and went through some of the new rules and regulations and a few exercises at a slightly gentler pace.

Phil is big, bald and scary. He drives a monster truck and looks as though he would eat 4th-team players for breakfast. Although he apparently sells stationery for a living, his appearance would suit him more for the role of henchman in a Guy Ritchie gangster movie. He had Tom, our nervy scrum half, practising his passing by attempting to throw balls through a lifebelt suspended in a metal frame at roughly fly half hand-height. Meanwhile the rest of us were made to roll around on the ground whilst he shouted the new tackling laws at us until our ears bled. I wasn't sure whether this was the kind of help we needed but after two seasons bouncing along the bottom of our league I was prepared to try anything.

I was also trying out a new direction in my career, having spun out of the charity world just as the sky was beginning to fall in on the economy. I was now working mostly from home, setting up a new consultancy company at possibly the worst moment in the economic cycle. It was good to escape the office politics by working for myself but it was tough trying to make a living. After long days staring at the walls and failing to generate any new business, training twice a week gave me a sense that I was doing something useful and added a little structure to my life. I also found a very supportive network at the club of other people at various stages of their careers offering advice, tips, contacts and a friendly ear to kick ideas around with. It was certainly preferable to sorting out my accounts or doing my tax returns.

Annoyingly, a few weeks into the season the politics of the rugby club seemed to rear its ugly head. The atmosphere at training started to turn a little sour and relationships between the coaches and leading members of the 1st team were not all they should have been. Instead of warming up by throwing the ball around and a few gentle stretches, Tuesday and Thursday evening sessions were preceded by strained meetings in the changing rooms throwing around grievances and complaints. A handful of the members of the squad had decided that they weren't getting what they wanted out of training. Sadly, what it turned out they were looking for was more 'contact'.

Contact is a delightful rugby euphemism. In any other context, 'contact' would be a nice thing. The chance for estranged fathers to take their kids out to the park and have an ice cream, an old friend getting in touch again after years on the other side of the world, a sensual massage from someone blonde and Scandinavian – you get the idea. But in rugby, more contact means grown men going out of their way to hurt each other in pursuit of the possession of a rugby ball. Now that is all very well in the context of an actual game of rugby on a Saturday afternoon, but in the middle of the week against people in your own club, with work the next day, it all seems a little unnecessary to me.

I made the mistake of attending one evening session, preceded by a particularly painful and awkward discussion which might just have usefully been about the varying shades of navel fluff for all the difference it had made. When it eventually came to an end, some rather frustrated and very strong 1st-team players jogged out to the training pitch with me and a couple of my bemused and bewildered 4th-team boys. After a token effort of a warm-up we were split into two groups and one half were pointed towards some padded 'tackle suits' – battered bits of foam encased in vinyl fabric offering no obvious protection that I could see. I should have walked away at that point and very nearly did. I was then supposed to help defend a small area of the pitch marked out by little plastic cones as a pack of drooling and snarling 1st-team grumpies practised rucking, mauling and generally hurting people. After five minutes or so of gratuitous violence I limped away battered and bruised, vowing never to return.

Things got worse on the following Saturday. A very solid opposition front row, with some unfathomable historic grudge against us, made a bit of a mess of my lower back, by lifting my upper torso up into the air in the scrum, whilst my second row tried to carry on pushing my lower half forwards. Two or three vertebrae and their associated muscles and tendons had an emergency meeting and decided to take industrial action, calling an immediate work to rule. I took myself off after about twenty minutes to negotiate with them, but rather foolishly went back on for the last ten minutes of the game without having reached a full and final settlement. By eight o'clock that evening I was unable to get off the sofa without assistance.

I couldn't really complain. I had got off quite lightly compared to our new recruit Richard.

John Waghorn and I had spotted Richard when he had come up to the club to buy some kit for his son. There are quite a few rugby dads out there who are just waiting to be asked to play. John noticed his prop-like stature and we induced him into the dark arts of the front row. Richard took the plunge and I was glad we had given him the opportunity to try out the game for himself. He made the mistake of telling his work colleagues, who quickly bought him an 'idiot's guide' book on rugby and booked their places on the touchline to watch his first and possibly only attempt at playing.

Alas, after an unfortunate encounter with an opposition boot, Richard ended up limping off the pitch after his debut appearance. It turns out that he had ruptured his Achilles tendon and had to have an operation to stick it all back together. We didn't see him at the clubhouse again.

The pitches were rock hard as there hadn't been much rain and I should have given my ageing body and those of my new charges a more thorough warm-up. I spent the rest of the week wincing in agony when trying to do anything remotely physically strenuous like putting on some socks or getting out of the car. What I really needed to do, I thought, was to start grooming a replacement, a body double for me and a new captain to take over for the next season. I needed to wean myself off this dangerous pastime, which was beginning to become no sport for old men.

Unable to stand up straight without the use of elephant-anaesthetising quantities of painkillers, I spent the next game on the touchline and handed the captaincy to Mark Bright. It was deeply frustrating not to be able to get on the pitch for what looked like a really tight game.

Our opponents Weybridge were from the higher of the two leagues merged to form the Surrey Foundation, so it would have been reasonable to expect us to be subjected to a general pasting. Instead, Brighty marshalled the troops well and kept us there or thereabouts for the full eighty minutes. We were competitive enough, and not only that but the team could cope perfectly adequately without me. This left me with mixed emotions. I would have liked to have been irreplaceably brilliant but also took a little pride in having put together a side that would continue to thrive should I end up under the Clapham Omnibus.

With consultancy work at home looking scarce I had, however, been offered an interesting project overseas. As a self-employed consultant I was loath to turn anything down, so for one week I would be running a media training session for new members of parliament in a ski lodge somewhere in the mountains of Macedonia. I was going to have to leave a bit more of the process of organising the team and captaining the side on the day to Brighty.

As a last act before flying off to the former Yugoslavian republic, I had gone to the selection committee. Minutes before it started I got the following shopping list by text from a keen Mark Bright who was taking his responsibilities very seriously, although not his spelling, punctuation or grammar.

```
SMS from Mark Bright 23 Nov 08:27
The squad I would love is front row your choice
waggers if you can. Mark gargner kearion schult ben
freeman joe yates Liam walker tom mcjennent matt
buckland shane smith ian bettsion Rory Bennent nick
Kewell chris lock & chapham. Danny gileaspe Simon
brown dan winfeild shane Webzell griggsy and me. Text
me when your chosing and I will call you
```

The pressure was on to select a decent side. We were up against one of the top sides in our league and unusually, due to opposition cry-offs and the odd win, we were actually in the top half of the table for the first time in our history.

SMS from Mark Bright 24 Nov 22:51
Has the squad been selected? Did we get everyone?

Mark really was keen. I had done my best with the other captains to give Mark a decent hand to start the week with but he was going to have to play well in the negotiations over the next few days to hang onto them all. Random players continued to text their availability to me during the week, keen to get involved in what was shaping up as an important home fixture.

SMS from Darren Dyer 25 Nov 9:09
Hi steve ill be there for the 2nd half mate ☺

Making sure that the Clapham city boys came was going to be crucial. Individually they were all quite handy but they tended to come as a job lot. It was all or nothing with them so Mark got to work on the Facebook page of one of their number. Tom McJennett is an advertising type with a creative approach to interpreting the rules of the game, which got him into trouble with referees most weekends.

Comments on Tom McJennett's Facebook wall:

Mark Bright: you are down for Sat are you bringing Ian?

Ben Hathaway: if u lot all play i'm keen - where is it, home ?

Mark Bright: it is a home game 230 kick off

Tom McJennett: me and Mike Tindall are playing - I am going to drive down if you want a lift down mate

Mark Bright: sounds good yes please

Ben Hathaway: yes pls - nice one

I texted my little brother Nathan to see if he could fill in for me. He hooked for his school 1st team and could play pretty much anywhere in the forwards. He was training to be a doctor, though, so it was always tricky to extract him from underneath a pile of medical journals or the opportunity to observe someone's internal organs being reorganised.

SMS from Nathan Gauge 25 Nov 13:30
I think i can this weekend-what are the times?macedonia sounds exciting

This was great news. The Clapham boys were big fans. I logged onto Facebook.

Me: My little brother Nathan is coming as my stunt double as I'm away in Macedonia - home win could put us joint top of the league!

Mark Bright: great news

Tom McJennett: what, great news that Steve is in Macedonia, bit harsh Brighty?!

Me: but fair

Ben Hathaway: who's going to give us an inspirational

half-time team talk ? McJennett you'd better get something
prepared

Clearly there was not much going on in the world of corporate
finance that afternoon. The banter continued as Ian Battison, one
of the city boys and a very handy centre, picked up on a slightly
sarcastic reference to him fancying himself as being in the same
league as England centre and royal consort Mike Tindall.

Ian Battison: Mike Tindall! Any guesses on the McJennett
penalty count on Saturday? I'm going for 7.

Tom McJennett: are you throwing your weight around Ian?

Back on the texts, Mark was having finger trouble during intense
negotiations with the 3rd-team captain.

```
SMS from Mark Bright 25 Nov 14:01
All sorted got a hooker now but steve is away so if
you need to swap players give me a text and we can
talk beers I might have a spare back
```

```
SMS from Mark Bright 25 Nov 14:01
Sorry Steve that was meant for redders
```

My email in-box was also filling up. The endless changing room
meetings had failed to resolve the existential angst being suffered
in the first team. A series of bad results had triggered off a flurry
of bad-tempered emails from committee members and blazer-

wearing benefactors. After some overenthusiastic use of the 'reply to all' function things had clearly got too much for the head coach who had apparently thrown his toys out of the pram. Dave Halliwell, the mighty second-row forward, who had sadly been sidelined with an injury for some time, piped up.

SMS from Dave Halliwell 25 Nov 14:51
What the fcuk is happening at the club? captain+coach
gone? the unmanageable wrfc curse. what about these
emails+team meetings? i'm just nosy like! hows u fella?

I reassured Dave that the 4ths were carrying on regardless of any bother the 1st team might be having. Whilst it was handbags at dawn in the upper echelons of the club, the atmosphere at the bottom was in good shape and I was keen to get Dave back on the field playing for us as soon as possible.

SMS from Dave Halliwell 25 Nov 14:51
glad to hear the 4s march on! will try to get up this
wkend to support. good luck!

SMS from Welcome 26 Nov 11:50
Virgin Mobile welcomes you to Macedonia. Calls cost
£0.60 per min to make and £0.30 per min to receive.
Texts cost £0.25. For help call +447953967967

Texts were expensive but they were a lot more interesting than the political game-playing that I was witnessing in our mountain retreat. My thoughts and reflections on the best ways to handle the modern media were being simultaneously translated to a group of MPs and parliamentary staff from the former Yugoslavian republic. They were listening politely but mostly because they had been told they couldn't join the EU unless they behaved themselves and looked like they wanted to become a proper democracy.

Phone calls were even more expensive and I was hoping that the funny noise you get when you try to call someone overseas would put off the older members of the squad like John Glover who preferred to use traditional communications to talk through the arrangements for the weekend fixture.

    You have a missed call from:
    John Glover

Interest was clearly growing in the fixture and Mark was now having to beat potential players away with a stick. Smelly Ben was trying to get a look-in.

    SMS from Ben 26 Nov 15:52
    Hi mate ben smith r u guys at home saturday

    SMS from Ben 26 Nov 15:54
    Good im gonna come up and cheer on the mighty fours

    SMS from Mark Bright 26 Nov 20:04
    Steve what are oppo or ref like with how many subs are
    used as we have a big squad now? we have lost keiran

```
and ben freemand but I have replacements so no biggy.
Do you want a text to say promotion is ours on sat
```

Mark now had so many players available that he was giving them away and it seemed for some reason John Glover really wanted to talk.

```
SMS from Mark Bright 27 Nov 9:54
Steve do you have chris lock and john taggarts mobile
as they have been promoted to the 3s and I need to
tell them


You have two missed calls from:
John Glover
```

Promoted to the 3rds was a bit of a euphemism. On the rare occasions we had too many players, only the ones we could live without were offered to the 3rd team. Chris and John were great lads, fully paid-up members of the Inbetweeners, but smaller than the rest of the squad and raised mostly on pick 'n' mix, they hadn't yet developed the muscle mass needed to survive in what was becoming the big fixture of the weekend.

Facebook again:

Dan Winfield's status:
Good luck with the rugby tomorrow lads sorry I can't be there! F**king work!

Danny Gillespie commented: screw work our biggest game of the season and you cry off

Dan Winfield commented: Dan I'm not happy about it mate.

SMS from Mark Bright 27 Nov 18:11
We might not have a game, Grant checked their website and has tried to contact them we will try again later. If they do show then I have a good team as not told people who I have will keep u updated have a good time

I urged Mark to hold his nerve. All the clubs at our level have occasional wobbly moments. This lot were top of the league and under gentle pressure from Grant, the club administrator, they would almost certainly honour the fixture.

SMS from Mark Bright 27 Nov 18:17
Cool no problem then I will text you with the win

Saturday morning, still in Macedonia and the texts started early:

SMS from Mark Garner 28 Nov 8:44
Sorry to bother you but lost Brighties number. What time is meet at club

SMS from Simon Phillips 28 Nov 9:21
Steve hope all is ok, who is in charge of 4s today? Simon phillips

SMS from Dan Winfield 28 Nov 12:24
Hey mate good luck today I hope you smash them. Let
me know how you get on

I turned my phone off, plugged in my translation headset and
settled in for another session on the finer points of post-cold war,
Eastern European politics. When I turned it back on during the
coffee break it fizzed into action again.

SMS from Dan Winfield 28 Nov 16:12
How did we get on mate?

SMS from Mark Bright 28 Nov 16:47
Sorry steve we lost 17-12 a try in the last 3 mins. The
hardest game they have played. We have had a vote
and your out and nathan is in.

My little brother had of course completely upstaged me as I knew
he would have done. I texted him for a little more detail.

SMS from Nathan 28 Nov 16:53
Hey steve, yeah it was good fun to get a runout, got
a good black eye and a sore neck! shame about the
result, just our fitness letting us down! they were
missing you a lot-said at the end of the game 'we've
done gaugey proud' soppy buggers! how was Macedonia

One of the Clapham boys hadn't lasted so well:

SMS from Matt B 28 Nov 17:03
Hi Steve, I dislocated my finger. Didn't even make it to
half-time! Probably won't be playing next week!!!!

SMS from Dan Winfield 28 Nov 17:11
Ah damn it. I'm available next Saturday.

SMS from Mark Bright 28 Nov 17:58
You should be very proud of all of them

And someone was still trying to get hold of me:

You have a missed call from:
John Glover

Chapter 20

Going the Extra Yard

It is well known that, in 1823, William Webb Ellis, with a fine disregard for the rules of the game as it was played at the time, first caught the ball and ran with it, thus creating the game of rugby. What is less well known is that when he was subsequently tackled a few yards short of the try line, he offloaded the ball to a young, dashing Ron Head.

Ron is still making himself available for selection at Warlingham Rugby Club in spite of the fact that he is largely held together with neoprene and gaffer tape. With a tiny frame and a thinning, silver-and-ginger comb-over, Ron turns out and limps around the pitch whenever given the chance. He is the only player I know who travels to fixtures using his OAP bus pass. Not only that but he is always happy to go in the front row, hooking or propping, and unbelievably seems to survive unscathed. Thanks to Ron I never had to field a 4th XV without a complete front row. Ron regards uncontested scrums as a fundamental violation of the human rights of a forward and will always step up to prop or hook if required.

Ron is actually a saint, who, with the long-suffering Mrs Head, has fostered and adopted a steady stream of severely disabled and disadvantaged children over many years. He had been unable to play for a few months following an operation and his wife was keen to keep him away from the rugby pitch and healthy enough to look after their highly dependent charges. For my next fixture, travelling away to Guildford, numbers were looking a little tight so I needed to call on Ron.

'I'll see what I can do,' he said.

Ron then hatched an elaborate plan for getting past Mrs Head and out onto the pitch. His kit had been left in his hallway by his front door for several weeks, whilst he hadn't been able to play. Leaving the bag there as a decoy, he craftily pulled together an alternative set of shorts, socks and strapping and hid it in his car whilst his wife wasn't looking. Come Saturday, when he told his wife he was 'just popping up to the club', she was reassured to see the original kitbag still in the hallway as he drove off. With his alternative kit and a mischievous grin he pulled into the car park alongside the rolling Guildford playing fields just in time to get changed and warm up before the kick-off.

With Ron's inspirational presence we also managed to show a fine disregard for the Surrey Foundation League form book and began to dominate the game. Otherwise petulant teenagers Kieran and Ben dramatically raised their game, recognising that someone old enough to be their grandfather was on the pitch and doing more than just making up the numbers.

Ron and I alternated between the positions of tight head prop and hooker. In spite of being half my weight and twenty years older, Ron outplayed me in both positions, locking out the scrum when he was propping and winning balls against the head whilst he was hooking. When I took my turn at propping I was pushed backwards by my opposite number on every scrum and ended up doing a little jig, like something out of *Riverdance*, in a desperate effort to stay upright.

A relatively new recruit, Danny Gillespie, also began to make an impact. A refugee from the association game, Danny is a dangerously good-looking builder with a successful business. He has an argumentative streak, presumably from years of experience of arguing with dodgy contractors on building sites around south London, which has given him the nickname 'Anger Management'. He kept his temper under control for this game and put his footballing skills to good use when he hacked at a loose ball and started the move in our own half that resulted in our first try.

Guildford play on public fields in an area called Stoke Park. Their pitch has what is known locally as a twenty-point slope. We had had the advantage of playing downhill in the first half, but when we swapped ends Guildford came back at us hard, scoring a succession of gravity-assisted tries. It looked as though our first-half lead would evaporate but then a handful of extra players appeared on our touchline. Delayed by traffic and teenage incompetence they had found their way to us when they probably ought to have been playing for the 3s or the 2s. They were very nippy around the pitch and grabbed us another couple of tries and sealed a rare 4th-team away win.

From this point onwards the momentum was with the 4th team and for the rest of the season we were nail-bitingly close to the top of our league. We won at home against South Godstone, where I even picked up another try using a tactic of hanging slightly off the pace until our scrum half Rory Bennett set off on a run. I then would chase him up the pitch, timing my run carefully so that when he got close to the try line, I was there to collect a pass and run the last few yards to the line.

We won at home against Racal Decca, a team that is linked to an old work social club for the radar and military electronics firm based in New Malden. Their skills of navigation were clearly well honed as they arrived for our fixture hours ahead of the kick-off and were warming up well before most of my players had even got out of bed. Fortunately teenagers Joe Yates and Chris Lock were on great form, or industrial-strength Red Bull, and towards the end of the game we were leading by twelve points to ten.

We looked like throwing the match away when, just before the final whistle, we conceded a penalty in a very kickable position. Not like the sort of thing that Jonny Wilkinson slots over, 45 metres away and hugging the touchline. This one was slap bang in front of the posts, 15 to 20 metres back, unmissable, or so we thought. Fortunately the Racal Decca World War Two target-sighting equipment was by now a little rusty and their kicker sliced the ball the wrong side of the posts.

Danny 'Anger Management' Gillespie was playing an increasing role in our success. With the zeal of a convert, this former footballer became an enthusiastic advocate for the 4th XV and a valuable recruiting sergeant. Passionately bothered about winning at almost any cost, he would fight for every ball and against any refereeing decision that got in his way. Opposition sides found him very easy to wind up and his hair trigger temper saw him get into the referees' bad book once or twice, but his level of commitment was unparalleled.

When I was next taken away with work, I left Danny in charge and he set about the task with gusto. In a series of expensive evenings in the clubhouse, he would challenge reluctant but talented players to a variety of complex bets. When eventually they lost the wager, their penalty was to play for him in the 4ths. He assembled a great side for the fixture against the 3rd XV from Old Blues, full of ex-1st-team players and fit, strong builders and labourers. Anyone who had ever lost a bet to him or who owed him a favour was dragged out onto the pitch. Old Blues, one of the oldest rugby clubs in the country, didn't know what had hit them. We won by a massive 40 points to 15. When I saw the result on my return to the country I knew I had found my replacement.

I've watched enough wildlife documentaries from the time when I worked at the Discovery Channel to know that once the alpha male in a group starts to age and show a few signs of weakness, the younger males fire up the testosterone levels and compete for dominance. As I let it be known that I was stepping down as 4th-

XV captain at the end of the season after three years in charge, the phenomenon so familiar to David Attenborough began to emerge.

Danny Gillespie, sniffing an opportunity in the air to take over the leadership of the pack, began to build up a following of powerful young bucks, who he continued to bribe, bully and cajole into turning out for us. The team that had once been the third-worst side in Surrey was now competing for one of the top spots in our league. Each week we either won convincingly or our opposition cried off the fixture and went in search of an easier and more relaxing way to spend their Saturday afternoon.

We even managed to coax the great David Halliwell, my bodyguard in the Purley John Fisher nose-crunching retribution incident, back out of a premature retirement to join in the fun. I had been pestering him to play every week with text messages and emails. Eventually he cracked, lured in by the prospect of a fixture against old rivals Mitcham, the side which had memorably taught me the rules about not handling the ball on the ground at the beginning of my rugby-playing career.

Rather than waiting for his long-term ankle injury to heal properly, David decided to play on with it anyway, and bought Boots out of their supplies of Tubigrip and surgical tape to hold the joint together. At our level of the game he could still make a valuable contribution by just turning up, looking massive and intimidating the opposition. He didn't really need to do a great deal beyond ambling gently from one scrum or line-out to the next and occasionally swatting aside anyone silly enough to try and start a fight. He was our own UN peacekeeping force and we were delighted to welcome him back.

The return of David Halliwell brought a few others out of the woodwork too. Lee, a former 2nd-team captain, and good friend of Dave's, came out of retirement. I had once driven Lee to East Surrey Hospital following an injury to his wrist after a match early in my rugby career. In those days the good-looking Lee was known throughout the club as Boy Band. Then he was a dashing back-row player combining speed around the pitch with teen idol good looks. Sadly now, a few seasons away from the pitch, he was a looking a little closer to Stavros Flatley than the boys from Westlife. He was clearly in need of a game or two.

We had twenty-seven men of various ages, all keen to show off what they could do in front of a noisy and enthusiastic home crowd. The Inbetweeners were getting bigger and stronger every week and it was with more than a little pride that I watched my young protégé, tiny Joe Yates, rampaging through the Mitcham defences, knocking players out of his way at will. DJ Reckless Shane Smith claimed a try, as did the boy-turned-man-mountain Kieran Scutt.

The Clapham boys combined to give their old school friend Matt a long-awaited run-out on the wing. Lining him up at the end of a beautiful set of passes, they gifted him the ball with a free run towards the try line. A few little winger's sidesteps would have seen him comfortably over the line, but unfortunately the passing years had turned him firmly into a prop, both in girth and mentality. He ran in a dead straight line into the arms of the first defender and was dumped firmly on the ground.

The testosterone levels were driven higher by the presence of David Halliwell's former politics teacher in the opposition back row. Released from the restraints of the classroom, where no doubt he was a mild-mannered and patient mentor, he spent the entire game ranting, raving and debating every decision as though it were prime minister's question time. Danny 'Anger Management' Gillespie was singled out for particular attention as the teacher offered extra tuition on his own particular interpretation of the laws of the game. Tempers rose and finally Sir resorted to a bit of corporal punishment, giving Danny a good old-fashioned clip round the ear. This gave Danny and the rest of us just the motivation we needed to step up our game a little more and score a few more tries.

We ended the game comfortable winners. It was a triumph. I no longer needed lessons in the rules from Mitcham and neither did my successor. Danny was blooded and ready to take over as captain and we ended the season third in the league. Not bad for a side that hadn't really existed three years earlier.

Fortunately, the increased levels of aggression during this time had been successfully directed towards our opposition and the occasional referee. The 4th-XV motto that I had drummed into my team, that no one gave anyone any sh*t for being sh*t, still held strong. We played in our last few games of the year like we had never played before. Instead of inventing excuses for playing badly I ended the season having to apologise to opposition captains for beating them so comprehensively.

As we celebrated the end of the season in the clubhouse, I took a look around and genuinely felt good about things. A few years earlier I had been deeply stressed and confused about life, work and everything. A random decision to take up a completely inappropriate sport had thrown me to the mercy of a bunch of pumped-up rugby-playing boys and men. I had learnt the game from scratch and had passed on something of its magic, culture and charm to a new generation of players. Even though I am only a mere 5 foot 6 inches, a few of these mammoth muscle-bound men seemed to genuinely look up to me.

'Nooooo... !'

Through the crowded bar I could see a long thin glass object filled with brown liquid working its way towards me. What had I been thinking? I snapped very quickly out of my sentimental self-satisfied smugness and realised to my horror I was going to have to do a yard of ale in a packed bar. There was no escape.

There are some people who can knock back large quantities of beer without it seeming to touch the sides. I suspect there is a simple genetic key that unlocks the ability to open the throat and poor alcohol in without needing to pause to breathe, swallow or eat a pork scratching. I simply don't have that gene. After painful training as a student, under the patient tutelage of a proper northerner and good friend Richard Pratt, I learnt to drink beer at a reasonably steady pace. Once in a while when I've had a thirst on, I have been known to be the first one to finish my pint in a normal, leisurely round of drinks, but competitive speed-necking of alcohol is not something I can do.

The fear of being forced to drink more than they want to is one of those things that put people off the game but, as I'd learned, it was reasonably easy to avoid most of the time. It had been quite liberating to discover that it was possible to just say no and still stay in and around the clubhouse and have a good time. The world has moved on and grown up and even in rugby clubs there was a little respect and restraint these days. It was OK to not drink and still be part of the game.

Mostly, that is.

On this occasion there really was very little I could do. Somehow I was going to have to consume two and a bit pints of foaming real ale in front of a crowd of baying rugby players. There was a slight risk that there might also be a few extra bits of detritus floating around in there too. Danny and his lieutenants had wanted to mark the end of my tenure as captain with a ritual humiliation, possibly to ensure that there was no way I would be tempted to cling on to the role for another year.

There were some immediate technical issues to be addressed. I was due to be collected in about half an hour or so by my wife and daughter to go out for a sophisticated meal for a family celebration. Every single previous act of yard drinking I had seen had involved considerable amounts of spillage, with victims pouring more down their front than into their mouths. So if I was to avoid spending the rest of the evening sitting in a restaurant smelling like a brewery I was going to need to take some evasive action.

Now I understand why there is so much public nudity associated with rugby and drinking. It is simply the most sensible practical response to a perfectly reasonable desire to minimise laundry costs and to enable the highest standards of sartorial elegance to be maintained. It seemed at that moment entirely logical to whip off my smart shirt and trousers that I had organised to wear for the outing later. I thought nothing whatsoever of standing on a chair in the middle of a crowded bar in my underwear. I was even quite pleased that I had decided to wear a decent pair of Paul Smith undies that I had picked up in an unusually extravagant airport purchase a few weeks earlier.

My only concern was that it was possibly going to take me ages to knock back this beer and there was a real risk that the rest of the bar might get a little bored waiting for me to gently sip my way to the bottom of the yard. There is only one thing worse than being humiliated in the middle of a bar with everyone staring and chanting at you, and that is being ignored as you are being humiliated in the middle of a bar, with everyone going back to their original conversations. Fortunately the sight of a middle-aged fat bloke in pink, stripey pants standing on a chair and dribbling beer down his vast belly was more than enough to keep them entertained.

So I steadily worked my way through the yard, urged on by the crowd chanting:

'Get it down, you Zulu warrior.
Get it down, you Zulu chief.'

If there had been any genuine Zulu warriors in the vicinity they would have been horrified to hear the wobbling pile of pink blubber in front of them being compared to the brave, noble tribesmen that fought so heroically to stand up to imperialist colonisation. Swiftly the singing switched to the slightly more appropriate alternative:

'Why was he born so beautiful?
Why was he born at all?

He's no f***ing use to anyone.
He's no f***ing use at all.'

I wasn't feeling terribly beautiful at this point but at least the volume of the beer was going down and it seemed to be staying down. I twisted the vase and got the last few dregs down my neck to a huge cheer from them and a massive sigh of relief from me. A combination of fear, adrenalin, peer pressure and public nakedness had helped me to get through the ultimate beer-drinking challenge. I could hold my head up high, although walking in a straight line was a little more of a problem.

Swiftly back into my clothes, I was never more relieved to be scooped up from the clubhouse by Mrs Gauge and whisked away for dinner with our daughter, convincing myself that I was entirely capable of holding a normal conversation and enjoying a very elegant dinner. I'm not sure I convinced anyone else.

Chapter 21

Look Back in Bognor

When doctors suggested that King George V might like to retire to the delightful Sussex seaside resort of Bognor, he is alleged to have cried out in anger the famous last words, 'Bugger Bognor,' before slipping away to his death. Several centuries later my 4th XV took this royal edict as an inspirational call to arms as we set off for our end-of-season tour.

Having blotted our copybook somewhat in East Sussex at Hellingly the previous year, we turned our attention to the bottom league in West Sussex when looking for a side to host our season finale. Chichester and Bognor both had sides competing in the brewery-sponsored Sussex 'Late Red' Division Three West and were conveniently placed close to the seaside. Enquiries were made and both sides initially came back to offer a fixture. Chichester eventually backed out, unable to raise a side or possibly because someone had tipped them off about the fixtures and fittings missing from Hellingly's clubhouse after the previous season's expedition.

Bognor is not only blessed with a beach and a rugby club. It also has a Butlins, a massive holiday camp packed with bars, nightclubs and cheap and cheerful accommodation. A quick phone call to a delightfully helpful Michaela in group bookings and I had secured twenty beds for two nights for such a ridiculously small amount that even the Inbetweeners would be able to afford to come along. Not only that, but Billy Butlin's heirs and successors were laying on something they referred to as a Big Weekend, with a selection of 1990s pop acts lured out of retirement by the prospect of performing to a packed crowd of drunken hen and stag dos from across the south-east.

I was ever so slightly nervous about this undertaking. It was complicated enough organising fifteen boys onto a rugby pitch for a couple of hours on a Saturday afternoon. As a grown-up, captain and representative of the club, I felt vaguely responsibly for their general health and well-being during a game and to some extent on their journey to and from wherever we were playing. Now I was going to have to babysit twenty of them for a long weekend with the added complication of alcohol, women, crazy golf and Redcoats.

All my players were, in theory, consenting adults, who in normal circumstances could be expected to conduct themselves appropriately in polite society. However, introduce a rugby tour into the equation, as I had discovered last year, and there is a powerful group dynamic at work which turns most participants into adolescent schoolboys, each competing to see who can be the biggest clown or can pull off the most outrageous prank. If anything went wrong, Michaela in group bookings knew where I lived and, more importantly, had my credit card details.

Just the simple mechanics of getting deposits and some contact details for the booking forms out of the lads seemed to take almost forever. The engaging, charming, boyish incompetence that is par for the course during the normal team activities throughout the year became deeply frustrating and financially troubling. I had a fiver here, a cheque there and an 'I'm-definitely-coming-but-I-just-need-to-get-to-pay-day' somewhere else. It was not helped by the fact that such information as I could glean about people's plans and intentions came to me late in the evening in the bar when I possibly had consumed one more beer than is recommended in the group holiday administrator's handbook.

Fortunately, my consultancy business was going reasonably well and I had been able to take on a delightful PA called Megan to help me keep on top of things. Organised, efficient and going out with the 1st-team full back (her initial interview for the job had taken place, I think, roughly two-thirds of the way through a club karaoke evening, sandwiched between my rendition of 'Stand by Your Man' and 'Mack the Knife'), Megan took over the booking arrangements. By cyberstalking the boys through their Facebook pages she extracted all the information we needed and paired them up into the twin rooms. Somehow, thanks to Megan's efficiency and Michaela's patience, I was handed a folder of beautifully organised booking confirmation sheets and an Excel spreadsheet that contained reassuring numbers indicating I might not be too much out of pocket at the end of the weekend.

There was only one other slight complication. I had managed to get some media management work for a chap who was the leader of a smallish political organisation that no one had really heard of: Nick Clegg, the leader of the Liberal Democrats. Young Mr Clegg at that time was struggling to be recognised amongst his own party members let alone the country as a whole. I was supposed to be schlepping round the country for the month before the General Election, twisting the arm of local newspaper reporters to persuade them to cover the opening of a crisp packet or some other non-event that I had managed to organise. Suddenly, after some funny little TV debates, something called Cleggmania took off (ah, those were the days) and I was in the middle of a massive media scrum, fending off requests from Korean broadcasters and NME reporters, and trying not to get impaled on the wrong end of a fluffy microphone.

The day before and immediately after the tour, I was supposed to be a calm, competent, media professional, effortlessly spinning stories around the biggest star of the General Election. This was possibly not the best time to simultaneously be responsible for a group of twenty drunken rugby players cavorting around a Butlins holiday camp.

I couldn't get out of either event and I couldn't let either group know about the other. I somehow had to get out of Butlins on Monday morning to nearby Southampton Hospital, clear-headed and with both my eyebrows still intact, to face the world's media, alongside the man who was going to become the Deputy Prime Minister. What could possibly go wrong?

We had arranged to travel independently to Butlins on the Friday to avoid the cost of a coach for the weekend. As I drove along the south coast, having said goodbye to my fellow spin doctors and the political pundits for the weekend, I picked up the first of many messages from Dave Halliwell, who was with a group that were making their way down by train. As I got nearer and nearer to Bognor, the messages from Dave got more and more exuberant and animated. By the time I finally arrived in the Butlins reception hall, still in my suit, I found a group of a dozen or so of the 4th XV, all decked out in matching navy-and-sky-blue-striped tour polo shirts, singing and chanting as they weaved their way to the group check-in. This was only about 5 p.m. I was very sober and they were very close to the opposite end of the scale.

I couldn't really disown them. They were chanting 'Gaugey is our Leader, Gaugey is our Leader' at the top of their voices. There could be no possible doubt whose fault they were. I checked them in as quickly as I could and went to my room relieved more than anything that Megan and Michaela had between them managed to sort things so that I had a room to myself. I had a small sanctuary where I could hide away with my laptop and mobile phone and pretend that I was a sophisticated communications consultant. I unpacked, took a deep breath and entered the fray to take what was coming to me.

An extensive statute book of tour legislation was introduced as we regrouped in one of the many bars a little while later. All drinks were to be held in the left hand throughout the weekend and were to be replaced on the table with a double tapping action. Anyone who was heard to comment, admiringly or otherwise, about any woman within eyeshot, could be instructed to 'tell her', and they would then have to make their feelings known to the person in question. Any violations of the rules were punished by a drinking forfeit, initially two fingers' worth of whatever was in your glass. This was rapidly amended by a 1st-team prop and legendary drinker known only as JD. He moved the 'When on tour, do four' clause, which was swiftly passed into law.

So, as you can imagine, I soon caught up with the blood alcohol levels of the rest of the group and in the end we had a thoroughly good-natured and entertaining night. There might have been a minor disagreement over the charging policy for a meal deal in the pizza takeaway but otherwise we were no worse than the hundreds of other groups of stags, hens and 30th, 40th and 50th birthday parties that were going on around us. In a sea of bizarre fancy dress costumes, the tour shirts helped us to find each other and stick together as we sampled the wide range of cheesy 1990s pop acts that had been laid on.

The next day was a little more complicated. On the face of it, all I had to do was get the boys up, into taxis and over to Bognor rugby club for a fairly civilised mid-afternoon kick-off. However, the journey from our hotel corridor to the taxi pick-up point just 500 metres away went past approximately seven separate bars. It was all I could do to keep the dishevelled rabble together without two or three sneaking off every 10 yards for a hair of the dog. The medicine of choice this morning turned out to be something called a 'Cheeky Vimto'. This is a cocktail made up of a couple of measures of port mixed with a blue WKD, and possibly some vodka, which bears an uncanny resemblance in flavour to the children's soft drink.

Worse than herding cats, the journey across the Butlins bar bonanza was more like herding a group of zombies with attention deficit hyperactivity disorder, each with a giant alcohol-magnet strapped to their forehead. Every few minutes two or three would wander off in search of fresh beer. Eventually I got all twenty out of the Butlins security gate, piled into a little heap of drooling, dribbling monsters and waiting for cabs. Five minutes was of course too long and by the time the cars arrived a couple of them had succumbed to the lure of the Cheeky Vimto and had been sucked back into the Butlins alcohol vortex.

Finally we got to Bognor's rugby club, to be greeted by the sight of a group of men in Hawaiian shirts and grass skirts mixing cocktails under a gazebo. It was a case of 'Out of the frying pan and into the fire'. Still, at least it wouldn't be just my players that would be incapable on the pitch. It wasn't long until the team hangovers were entirely replaced by new levels of inebriation. Finally, just as we were ready to start playing, we were treated to the spectacle of one of the Bognor team members being sent off to run around the entire pitch wearing nothing but a bright green mankini. Who needs national anthems or the All Blacks' haka when you can have a drunken, near-naked Borat impersonator as your pre-match ritual?

The game itself turned out to be surprisingly serious with a fair bit of niggle and aggression on both sides. I mostly took cover behind Dave and Lee who co-ordinated defences as best they could. We had a surplus of front row so I sent the first-team prop

Scotty, who had come along for the ride, to play at full back. There he waited patiently until Bognor kicked the ball to him. This was something he had clearly been looking forward to all season. Props don't often get the chance to run with the ball, being kept back for the pushing and shoving involved in the scrums, rucks and mauls. Once he got a little speed up, Scotty's momentum saw him bashing his way through the Bognor defences in an almost unstoppable rampage.

The only unfortunate incident in the game was a minor altercation with Bognor's Borat lookalike, who had foolishly opted to play in his novelty underwear. He had somewhat upset Lee 'Boy Band' Braysher by throwing himself into a ruck a little too enthusiastically and smothering the ball. The argument was very quickly settled in our favour as Boy Band hoisted baby Borat up by the straps of his mankini, generating the world's worst ever wedgie, and raising the poor boy's singing voice high enough to take the falsetto parts in Lee's pop combo.

After the game Bognor were, of course, wonderful hosts, feeding us well and entertaining us in their bar. It turned out that they had entirely endorsed and approved our treatment of their mankini wearer, who had apparently been getting on their collective nerves all season. We exchanged club memorabilia and reflected on our respective seasons, the state of our clubs and our general shared love of the game. Their chairman had even organised a magician who wandered around performing close-up sleight-of-hand tricks, which would have been confusing enough had we been sober, but drunk as we were we began to seriously question the laws of physics as we had previously understood them.

What a treat. To have pinged off a random email almost on a whim a few months earlier and then, as a result, to have been looked after so well by a group of complete strangers in a little clubhouse by some playing fields. Something about the game of rugby seems to make this happen. Go into any clubhouse and you will see plaques and other ornaments dotted around the walls as a memorial to fixtures like this one played between clubs from all over the country and all over the world. Men, who as a species are generally a fairly grumpy and uncommunicative lot, sharing a common love of a great game with gentlemen from all walks of life and all corners of the globe. A little sporting competition, some modest reciprocal violence and aggression, followed by some reciprocal hospitality and genuine human warmth.

As the sun began to set over the Bognor playing fields, we said our goodbyes and piled in taxis back into the bacchanalian orgy that is the Bognor Big Weekend.

Feeling full of love for one's fellow man, where else could anyone want to be but at an S Club 7 gig in Bognor? The 1990s themed weekend was reaching its pinnacle with a headline slot for the shiny, happy TV teenage drama series band that lifted the hearts of a generation and led us out of that difficult decade and into a new millennium filled with optimism and hope. Well maybe something like that.

S Club 7 had now been reduced to S Club 3, but the key elements were still there: Jo, the one that could sing a bit but couldn't manage to live in a televised house full of celebrities without getting drawn into a bullying scandal with racial overtones, was in fine voice. Bradley, the one who could rap and dance a bit, did his thing and was clearly unphased by his bandmate's Big Brother antics. The third member of the troupe was Paul, who was no doubt lovely and charming in his own way, but I wasn't entirely sure I recognised him. He looked perhaps as though he might be more at home in our front row than at the front of the stage. According to his Internet biographies, he did once harbour a desire to be a professional rugby player so, Paul, you know where to find us.

Using all our scrummaging skills, giant second row Dave Halliwell, first-team prop Scotty and I squeezed our way through the crowd of fifteen-year-old girls so that we were in touching distance of the stage. In what was possibly the most bizarre and surreal night in all my forty-four years to date, I celebrated the end of my last season as captain of the Warlingham 4th XV with two huge rugby forwards, dancing and singing along to the three survivors of S Club 7, reaching for the stars, climbing every mountain higher, following my heart's desire and discovering that it is indeed true that there ain't no party like an S Club party. Quite what the teenage girls that made up the bulk of the audience thought of us, I can't imagine.

Naturally we popped round to the stage door to have a chat with Jo and the boys, although for some unfathomable reason they seemed a little confused and bewildered at the sight of a portly little middle-aged hooker, fresh from one game of rugby and the best part of twenty-four hours drinking, wanting to discuss with them how through their music they had spoken for a generation. Either that or Jo was distracted by the devilish good looks of the second-row player standing behind me. There is something in a cauliflower ear that turns the girls wild, I'm told.

Inspired and rejuvenated by S Club and fuelled by more and more alcohol, the weekend continued at this ridiculously euphoric pace. I discovered that within five minutes, with one group text, I could summon at least a dozen navy-and-sky-blue-striped rugby players onto any one of the many Butlin's dance floors. Kieran showed off his party trick of lifting consenting young women into the air with one arm. The better-looking backs tried talking to them. Inevitably we spent a little time in the karaoke bar, adding some volume and bass notes to the community singing. I sang a duet with someone dressed as a Care Bear, which seemed entirely appropriate. In any other circumstances, similar behaviour by someone my age would have me delivered swiftly into the care of the local authorities.

Remembering the day job, I opted for a tactical retreat on the last night and managed to get back to the relative safety of my room reasonably early and reasonably sober, as the rest of the boys partied on. By the next morning I was back in a suit and herding Lib Dem activists into a huddle around their leader. After the excesses of the weekend, managing the media scrum was like a gentle walk in the park. I was still humming S Club 7 tunes quietly to myself as Nick and his battle bus rolled on to their next destination.

For me the highlight of the tour had been when we managed a choral team rendition of a hastily rewritten version of the nineties classic Oasis tune, 'Don't Look Back in Anger'. John Glover hadn't joined us on the tour this year, but he featured in the chorus. For the record, and with apologies to Liam and Noel, here is the Warlingham 4th-XV reinterpretation:

Don't Look Back in Bognor

Slip a short inside of your pint
Don't you know you won't find
A better place to play
You said that you'd never been
But all the tours that you've seen
Are gonna fade away

So I start to do selection from my bed
Cos you said the team I had went to my head
Step outside, the referee's in gloom
Bend down and do up your lace
Wipe that mud from off your face
Cos you ain't ever gonna run my heart out

So Glover can wait, he knows he's too late
And he's running the line
The ball's kicked away, but don't look back in Bognor
I heard you say

Take me to the pitch where you go
Where nobody knows
How you're gonna play
Please don't put your life in the hands
Of a middle-aged man
Who'll throw it all away.

So I start to do selection from my bed
Cos you said the team I had went to my head
Step outside, the referee's in gloom
Bend down and do up your lace
Wipe that mud from off your face
Cos you ain't ever gonna run my heart out

So Glover can wait, he knows he's too late
And he's running the line
The ball's kicked away, but don't look back in Bognor
I heard you say

Repeat last verse x 2

... Least not for Gauge

Chapter 22

The Art of Not Tackling

Freed up from the burdens of captaincy, I was now freed up to work on improving my own game. As the next season approached I decided to see if I could turn myself, at the ripe old age of forty-three, into a half-decent player. I had been bumping along, making up the numbers for several seasons. With Danny Gillespie captaining the 4th team I could expect the games to have a more serious competitive edge and it was going to be a struggle to keep my place. Danny had a genuine winning instinct and was going to expect a little more than for me to just turn up and play.

I even started to harbour vague fantasies about benching for the 1st team for just one game. Over the years I had spotted that towards the end of every season the 1st team seemed to start to struggle for players, especially if there was no chance of promotion or winning their league. Injuries take their toll over the course of a year and a few players have the will to play battered out of them over a gruelling season. There had been odd occasions when they were so short for numbers that genuine 4th-team players had been asked to step up and play in order to honour a fixture. Funnily enough, though, they had never quite got desperate enough to ask me.

The one area of my game that was seriously deficient was tackling. At this stage in my career, after about seven seasons of playing, I could count the number of successful tackles I had made on the fingers of one KitKat. Tackling is a vital part of the game and my inability to stop other players has probably contributed to more tries being scored against us than any other single factor. Once opposition sides worked out that I couldn't stop them, their players would run at me all afternoon, knowing that they would almost certainly score.

Tackling is one part of the game that does not appear to be taught once you get past about thirteen. Prepubescent rugby-playing boys are lined up by eager coaches and taken through the elements of a perfect tackle step by step. They start by learning how to fall safely, tucking their arms out of harm's way and collapsing onto the fleshier parts of their anatomy. They then shuffle towards each other on their knees, going through the motions of a tackle, but with less far to fall. Building up through walking pace to jogging and finally to running, they slowly work out where to put their head to avoid getting hurt as they bring down their opponents.

Small boys also spend their school lunch breaks, when they can get away with it, playing slightly more violent versions of British Bulldog and develop an immunity to fear and a slightly thicker skull.

By only really starting to play the game properly in middle age, I had missed this crucial stage in my rugby development and as a result I have struggled to grasp this area of the game. My little brother Nathan had done his best to point me in the right direction when I first took up the game but I had never really mastered it. Instead I had perfected the delicate art of 'not tackling'. This is a far more intricate, technical performance than you might imagine. First of all you have to make sure that whenever possible you are nowhere near any opposition players running with the ball. This requires a careful reading of the flow of the game and an occasional, confident jog to the opposite side of the pitch to avoid any likely forthcoming attack.

In the event that an opponent carrying the ball does appear in your vicinity, you need to time your approach very carefully, in order to look as though you are making every effort to reach him, without actually getting into tackling range. As you get close-ish you can perhaps make a vague lunge in his direction with an outstretched arm, whilst keeping your other limbs and vital organs safely out of harm's way.

Finally, you will need to embark on an heroic pursuit after people who are clearly already through your side's defences and almost certain to score a try. No one will expect you to catch them, but it looks as though you are showing willing. This is an entirely futile exercise but it does help to keep you fit and has the added benefit of reducing the risk of injury.

At all times you have to avoid the possibility of an opponent running directly at you. If this happens the only way to avoid tackling them is to step sideways out of their way and it is hard to make that look anything other than pathetically cowardly.

The game that made me finally decide to do something about my abysmal tackling was the 4th-team fixture against Merton. Under Danny's leadership we were close to the top of our league and looking forward to finally beating what had been a bogey team for us for several seasons. The game itself, however, was a bit of a disaster. Their prop, Ming the Merciless, was making life difficult in the scrums and then my progress towards benching for the 1st team by the end of the season took a serious step backwards.

One of the jobs of being a hooker is a simple defensive task during line-outs when the opposing side is throwing the ball in. There is a 5-metre gap between the touchline where the attacking hooker stands to throw in the ball and the first man in the line-out, usually a big, fat, slow prop. The defending hooker's job is to stand a little way back guarding that 5-metre channel and make sure that no one with the ball comes through that space. It turns out to be remarkably rare for any attacking player to try and get through that gap. Normally someone catches the ball, perhaps forms a little maul and then gets the ball to the scrum half, who passes it in the other direction, away from the touchline and towards the middle of the pitch, where speedy backs are waiting with their hands out for the ball. I have happily occupied the channel by the touchline for many seasons without really having to do anything much other than look big and fat and vaguely interested.

Unfortunately, on this occasion Merton had a canny hooker who had other plans and had worked out a little move with his fellow forwards before the game. It was nothing terribly sophisticated but it was not something we usually came up against. The hooker threw the ball to the jumper at the front of the line-out who then, instead of passing it to the scrum half or dropping down and starting a maul, threw the ball straight back to the hooker. This caught me completely unawares, even though it was exactly the sort of thing I was supposed to be there for. The hooker ran straight towards me, in perfect tackling range.

The Merton hooker hadn't built up any great pace by the time he got to me but with a decent-sized belly, he had a little bit of momentum. I unfortunately had nothing to offer in the way of a tackle and just flapped my arms vaguely at him as he ran straight through to score a try. It was utterly humiliating and even worse was that he did exactly the same thing a few minutes later.

My only consolation was that I managed to prevent him from picking up a hat-trick, by somehow stopping him on the try line just before the final whistle. This might have had more to do with the fact that Dave Halliwell had nearly killed him a few minutes earlier with a massive hit that left him doubled up and wheezing on the ground for about five minutes. I also needed Joe Yates, probably the smallest other player on the pitch, alongside me to provide some bulk.

I decided to sort myself out some remedial tackling practice. It was all a bit too embarrassing and odd to approach the 1st-team coaches and our previous 4th-team coach Phil had gone back to shouting at paper manufacturers. I needed to get creative and look further afield.

Conveniently, a fit, keen young trainee PE teacher was spending a lot of time around the club and seemed like the sort of person who could help. This was someone who had played a lot of rugby at a neighbouring club and was a ferocious tackler. Fresh from a placement at an inner city secondary school, I thought that they would have the patience and educational skills to get something of the tackling techniques programmed into my late-developing rugby brain. The only possible issue that might cause a problem was that in this most macho of sports my prospective, remedial tackling coach was – a woman.

Sophie was, however, more than happy to take me on. I suspect she might have been able to skip the special needs modules of her teacher training course as a result. To avoid any risk of awkward grappling moments we also recruited one of the Inbetweeners, Ben Freeman, to act as a tackle bag and chaperone. The next Monday evening Sophie had me running up and down alongside the netball pitches, and crunching my shoulder repeatedly into Ben's impressive six-pack.

It took a little while to unlearn all my well-honed tackle-avoidance strategies, like waving my arms around like a wind turbine. I also had a habit of running very quickly and keenly towards people with the ball, only to slow down at the last moment in order to avoid contact. After what felt like an hour, but was probably more like twenty minutes, of tackle after tackle on the unflinching Mr Freeman, I was beginning to get the hang of it.

Tackling is apparently all about momentum. If you have more of it than your opponent you will probably come off better in any tackling encounter. Physics was never a strong point of mine but I am reliably informed by my fifteen-year-old son that, according to his GCSE textbooks, momentum is equal to mass times velocity. I was doing alright as far as the mass goes, years of consuming coronary-inducing quantities of beer and chips having done their job, but summoning up any sort of velocity was still proving to be a bit of a challenge.

My favourite second-row player ever, David Halliwell, has got this physics thing well and truly sorted. By being fairly massive, he doesn't really need to generate much velocity in order to get the better of an opponent. A gentle jog into the impact and he will normally wipe out anyone even if they are running at full pace. He also seems to be able to call on one other little bit of physics; gravity. I played one game with him in Hastings and we were generally doing quite well. However, the opposition seemed to have one decent player who was running rings round us. I decided, as you sometimes do in these situations, to take exception to the manner in which he was relishing his success at nipping around the field, handing off tackles. To be honest, he had smirked once too often and, frankly, I thought that was dashed unsporting. Not that I was going to do anything about his behaviour myself, you understand. That would be going too far. What's more, he was a lot bigger than me. However, I suggested to David that he might want to see what he could do.

Within a few minutes the arrogant-looking Hastings back-row player set off on another humiliating little run, but got a little too close to Mr Halliwell. Instead of running round him, he seemed to be sucked in closer to the great man, like a little asteroid being pulled off course by a large planet. David lined himself up for the impact with a gentle step forward and that was enough to create the momentum advantage. With a huge thud the Hastings player was flattened and the annoying grin was very much wiped off his face.

The surprising thing I discovered in my remedial training session with Sophie and Ben is that tackling doesn't actually hurt as much as it looks like it ought to. If you can line your shoulder up with a reasonably soft bit of your opponent and keep your head on the right side of their body, it turns out to be relatively painless. I began to look forward to the opportunity over the rest of the season to try out my new skills and see if I could make a more useful contribution in defence once in a while.

I didn't get much of a chance. The season was dogged by massive snowfalls and fixture cancellations. On the odd occasion when we could find an unfrozen pitch we struggled to find an opposition to play against. Under Danny's leadership we were almost unbeatable and week after week our opponents seemed to find better things to do with their Saturday afternoons. Perhaps, I fantasised, they had heard about my new tackling training with Sophie and Ben and they were anxious to avoid being on the wrong end of a big hit from me.

The lack of 4th-team fixtures didn't mean that I sat at home watching the television. Instead I spent several Saturday afternoons running up and down the touchline with a flag, as a touch judge for the 3rd-XV fixture, only occasionally getting onto the pitch for the last few minutes or earlier if someone got injured.

The more I hovered around the fringes of the higher sides, the more I thought I could perhaps have a crack at benching for the 1sts at some point towards the end of the season if I kept improving my game. Then an opportunity came my way to impress the chairman of selectors with my developing ability and line myself up for an end-of-season slot as a 1st-team supersub. Mark O'Connor, who had recently taken over the task of picking the 1st team in conjunction with the coaches, was also planning to have a run-out with the 3rds. Mark is an enthusiastic second-row player who enjoys jumping in the line-out and was running through some drills with the 3rd-team forwards before a game. Seizing the opportunity to show my keenness and growing confidence I offered to have a go at lifting him in the line-out, making myself, so I thought, a little more selectable. Normally at line-outs my job was to throw the ball in, but the 3rd team already had a dead-eyed thrower in the side. My only way of being useful was to try the lifting job.

We went through the codes and I lined up behind Mark, bent down and tried to work out which bit of the back of his legs to grab hold of. Trying hard to keep my thumbs from going anywhere unpleasant I held onto the top of his thigh and the bottom of his shorts as Mark leapt into the air to catch the ball. Getting him up in the air turned out to be relatively straightforward; a doddle in fact. Bringing him safely back down again turned out to be a little more tricky. Mark wriggled and twisted out of my grasp and fell a bit too quickly onto the ground. He landed awkwardly and let out a loud scream. As he hobbled off in search of physiotherapists and ice packs, my chances of making it into a 1st-team shirt shrivelled to less than zero. I picked up my flag and went back to the touchline.

I was beginning to feel my age too. The injuries from the previous season didn't seem to have properly healed and new ones were acquired on top. I even suffered the indignity of being overlooked in favour of the significantly older John Glover as he was brought on from the bench before me during one 3rd-team game.

There is an ongoing battle of the generations in rugby as older chaps desperately try to cling on to their youth and younger players try to assert themselves and claim a higher slot in the rankings. I began to feel I might be on my way down, but whilst people like John Glover and Ron Head were still playing, I was not going to bow out just yet.

Whilst I wasn't playing at my best, there were a couple of victories for the wrinklies in a fixture against Old Paulines. One of the veterans running out with the 3rds was Shane Webzell. One of the more senior players in our club, he was desperately fit having just returned from ascending Mount Everest on a unicycle or some such sponsored stunt. We were all tiring towards the end of the game when we were awarded a penalty within our own twenty-two. Shane, keen to take advantage of a little confusion amongst the opposition, opted to take a quick tap penalty. He then set off on an enthusiastic little run, with memories no doubt flooding through of his younger speedier days, before the opposition had managed to retreat the required 10 yards. The Old Paulines players were a law-abiding lot and so left Shane untackled as he ran on through their ranks. This was all very well but Shane too was a little weary and so took a detour, heading directly towards one of the nearest opposition players, bumping into him and virtually forcing the player to make an illegal tackle. The referee blew the whistle and Shane earned another penalty 10 yards up the pitch having only had to run for 5 of them.

The highlight of the whole game came courtesy of little Matt Robinson, a supremely confident scrum half and fully paid-up cast member of the Inbetweeners. It had always been a joy to watch Matt play, especially when he had the ball and set off on a cheeky run through the opposition forwards. However, this was not his finest hour. In the last few minutes, in a game where tackling had not been our strong point, Matt was our last line of defence against an opposition player running at him at some pace. The Old Paulines man was indeed old, not old by Ron Head/John Glover standards, but certainly thinning up top and looking a little lived-in.

'Come on, old man,' called the young number 9 as he psyched himself up for the tackle, possibly not realising he was speaking out loud. The old man in question took one withering look at Matt, and with a flick of his Zimmer frame, stepped round the shamefaced young back and ran off to score yet another try. With my Alzheimer's setting in I can't quite remember the final score, but in my mind it remains one-nil to the wrinklies.

When I eventually got a 4th-team fixture it was against our old friends from Croydon. Danny had too many good-quality players to choose from, so once again I spent the first half with the linesman's flag on one touchline and John Glover spent it with the bucket of water and magic sponge on the other. Fortunately, by half-time Danny and his young bucks had organised a decent lead and he felt confident to bring on the old lags. Croydon, however, saw this as an opportunity to regroup and so the game got a little more intense and competitive as a result.

The way the game was shaping up it looked like we were going to need to defend a bit and I might be called upon to show that

I had learnt something from my remedial tackling lessons. After a period of scrappy play where the packs of opposing forwards exchanged short little runs at each other, I saw my chance. One of the smallest and oldest Croydon players came running towards me with the ball. He was going slowly enough and his escape options were limited by the crowded corner of the pitch we were in. Surely even I could stop him.

I set myself up for the impact, remembering what Ben and Sophie had taught me, lowered my centre of gravity and set the Croydon senior citizen in my sights. I told myself that he was going down. In fact he did go down, or rather he dipped his head down and charged straight towards me, picking up his speed as he hurtled in my direction. I couldn't get any lower. My arthritic knees wouldn't bend any more than they already had. Now I had nowhere to go and the psychotic granddad clattered his thick hard skull straight into the middle of my ribs.

I had sort of stopped him, in that he didn't run any further on that particular attack and at least I hadn't stepped out of the way as I might have done previously. However, the moral victory was with the Croydon granddad as I was in lots of pain. His front-row colleagues then spent the rest of the game playfully headbutting me in every scrum after that. I was going to need to take a little more care and invest in some better body armour if I was going to survive in this game for very much longer.

Chapter 23

Champions?

I can normally measure how tough a game of rugby has been by seeing how long it takes to put on my socks on the following Sunday morning. After the 4th-team game against Croydon it took until about Tuesday lunchtime. I waddled around like an incontinent ninety-year-old for days. The Croydon player's head bone had connected to my rib bone and that rib bone was connected to my backbone. For much of the following week, anyone near me could hear the name of the Lord taken in vain as I blasphemed in pain every time I moved. I wanted to get back on the pitch but for several weeks afterwards my back simply failed to work as a back is supposed to.

Injuries in rugby are part of the game. Most clubhouses will have someone hobbling around on crutches or carrying an arm in a sling somewhere or other after every game. Pulled ligaments and broken bones are commonplace and no one seems particularly phased by them. Some take a peculiar pride in their sprains and ailments, spending hours in physiotherapy or being scanned and operated on from one season to the next.

I had managed reasonably successfully to keep out of trouble for most of the time I played. The forwards' part of the game may look terrifying, but for much of the time the contact is controlled and predictable like in the scrum and at the line-out. Even in loose play the game is played at fairly close quarters and so it is rare for anyone to get much momentum going, so the impact when it happens is relatively tame. Taking into account the layers of padding around the midriffs of the men in the lower divisions of the game, you can see how the risks are minimised.

One of the few times I had been hurt was when I was playing out in the backs. In a game against Crawley early on in my career I had been stuck out on the wing by a captain who, I suspect, didn't really want me on the pitch at all. Although I was a long way away from the play and out of harm's way for most of the game, when the ball did eventually come in my direction it was accompanied by a fast, bony opposition player with a clear sense of purpose. With the wider open spaces in the bits of the pitch where the backs play, my opponent had gathered a lot more speed than I would normally encounter. He may have been a lot smaller than a forward but his light, angular frame did more damage to me than any of the rounded, lumbering props and second-row players that I normally bump into on the pitch ever did.

It is always the tougher, fitter players that end up getting injured.

They are the ones who have the energy to get to every breakdown or need to be tackled by the opposition. If you are not all that good at the game, it is fairly hard work to get hurt. You really need to know what you are doing in order to break something serious. For most of my rugby-playing career I had dodged serious injury.

So it was deeply frustrating as the 4th XV set off on a serious championship challenge that I was forced off onto the sidelines with debilitating back pain. Danny was leading the team to beat all-comers, whereas I had to settle for a series of exhausting stretches and exercises to try and get my back working again. I seemed to spend hours every day lying on my back and pulling my knees into my chest or on all fours alternately arching and flexing my spine. The latter manoeuvre was the sort of move you might see performed by a bootilicious babe by a Hollywood poolside in a rap star's pop video. I don't think my bellylicious version as practised on the living room carpet would quite make the cut.

The physio insisted that there was nothing fundamentally wrong with me. My muscles had gone into some sort of spasm but they were really just being overcautious. All they needed was some gentle reassurance that everything was well and they would relax and let me move once again. I steadily worked through all the stretches I had been given to do at home and gradually began to free up one or two vertebrae. For a little while I was able to move almost normally. Then I did something mildly strenuous like attempt to dunk a ginger biscuit in a cup of tea and my back seized up all over again. This happened again and again.

There was one big crunch game looming and I was desperate to get fit in time for it. Sutton and Epsom 6th XV were the only thing that stood between us and the Foundation League Championship. They had won all their games so far this season and were always formidable opponents. They were due to come to us and whoever won would almost certainly win the league. It was going to be a massive game.

My back was touch-and-go all week in the run-up to the fixture but I was determined to play. On the morning of the game I carefully stretched every muscle I could identify in my back and then ladled half a ton of Deep Heat onto any of the bits I could reach without setting it off again. I got to the clubhouse early and changed incredibly carefully, making sure I did nothing that could possibly set off those touchy back muscles into another silly spasm. Hanging off behind the rest of the team during the warm-up I jogged around slowly, taking great care, and avoided the usual little pre-match game of touch rugby that we played just to get used to catching the ball.

Danny Gillespie eventually clocked that I was clearly not anything like a hundred per cent fit as I tentatively tiptoed around the pitch. This was a massively important fixture for Danny and the whole team. He had put a huge amount of effort into getting the 4ths into the position where we could win the league and he was not one to risk throwing that opportunity away. He had very sensibly taken the precaution of recruiting another hooker, who looked an awful lot stronger and younger than me. As I winced my way through yet another set of back stretches I thought I would be out of the game.

The captain wandered across and asked how I was doing. We both knew I shouldn't play but we both knew how important this game was to me too. I had spent three years creating the 4th team out of next to nothing. It wasn't so much a team, it was more a way of life. Every weekend we created an event that wouldn't have happened otherwise. Something like a hundred different people had played for us over the years. Each of them had become part of a little corner of the club and a part of the sport with its own culture and sporting ethos. A team where no one gave anyone any sh*t for being sh*t. A team where everyone and anyone could play. Old men, teenagers, fat men, thin men, quick men, slow men and one grumpy middle-aged back-spasming man.

Danny should have told me to put on my tracksuit to keep warm on the touchline whilst he made sure his alternative hooker knew all our line-out calls. Instead he asked me what I wanted to do and let me make the decision whether to play or not and whether I should be in the starting line-up. I put my mouthguard in and got out onto the pitch, waiting for the referee's whistle to start the game.

It was a tough first twenty minutes. Both sides were utterly determined and the rucks and mauls were hit at a ferocious pace. Sutton and Epsom were a well drilled side that had clearly played together for some years. They even had a chap on the touchline with a clipboard, showing levels of administrative efficiency rarely seen in the Surrey Foundation League. Their training-ground moves were executed smoothly and alternate game plans were no doubt deployed but somehow we managed to hold off the onslaught.

With the adrenalin, pride, Deep Heat and ibuprofen coursing through my veins I managed to stay on the pitch and just about hold my own. I was able to do my share of pushing and shoving, clearing opposition players out of rucks and adding some weight to our attacking mauls. Comfortably nestled between the two props in the front row I was able to hook the ball out of the middle of the scrums without sending my back off to painful spasms again.

We were holding our own against the league leaders Sutton and Epsom, a team that had beaten us comfortably so many times in previous seasons. Their usual ageing and moustachioed fly half who looked like Errol Flynn had been left on the touchline as they had clearly brought a good collection of younger, stronger players with them for this crucial fixture. Their chap with the clipboard was making furious notes and barking instructions from the touchline.

I was just about keeping up but a little off the pace. Ahead of me, about a third of the way into our half, the bulk of the forwards were scrabbling around for the ball. Taking a bit of a breather I hung back in the defensive line waiting to see what would happen. Then, all of a sudden, one of their forwards, a powerful-looking back-row player, broke away clutching the ball. He was running straight towards me, the worst tackler on the pitch with a deeply dodgy back. If he got past me, he would almost certainly score and we would be on the back foot and our chances of winning the league would evaporate.

In normal circumstances I would try some of my not-tackling techniques: running towards him but not close enough to reach him, waving my arms around about or just stepping out of the way. But this game was different. I was keeping a much better player on the touchline. I needed to justify my existence. I braced for impact.

Meanwhile, back where all the other forwards were, Danny 'Anger Management' Gillespie had clearly upset someone. As a result, one of the Sutton and Epsom players decided to thump Danny. The rest of the Warlingham forwards leapt to his defence and within moments a full-on brawl had broken out.

The chap with the ball was oblivious to what was going on behind him. He kept on his relentless path towards me as the nerve endings in my back began to get wind of what was about to happen. Cowering in fear, I edged my shoulder towards the rampaging attacker. He really didn't look like he was going to stop. Every sensible instinct in my brain was screaming at me to get out of the way, but I had a job to do for Danny, for the 4ths, for all the people who had coached me and selected me for their sides over the years. I was going to stop this guy if it was the last thing I did. I planted my studs firmly in the ground, dropped my shoulder and braced for the impact. He crashed into me and the shock went straight from my shoulder and sent the muscles in my lower back into the twitching spasming agony they had been in all week long. My back, though, had done its job. I now had to use my arms to try and grab hold of him and hang on as best I could. I tried to manoeuvre enough of the rest of my bulk to block his path and reduce his speed. All the while, I was waiting and hoping I could hang on to him long enough for someone else to arrive and stop him completely.

And then I heard the sweetest sound. The referee blew his whistle to stop the twelve-man fight that had broken out on the other side of the pitch. I had done just enough to slow down the potential try scorer. Danny Gillespie's eminently punchable face had done the rest. The defence had held for just long enough, and my back had held out just long enough, to make a bit of a difference.

I crawled off to the touchline but I had done my job. I had absorbed some of Sutton and Epsom's initial impact and whilst Danny had been receiving a bit of anger management therapy from the opposition, I had stopped a try. Danny's younger, stronger hooker jogged onto the pitch, fresh as a daisy and slowly the game started to swing our way. The pain in my back subsided as I watched my friends run in try after beautiful try. We were twenty points ahead, then thirty, then forty, then fifty. Sutton and Epsom had completely lost their momentum and possibly their will to live. Not even bringing on their Errol Flynn lookalike at fly half could turn around their fortunes. By the end of the match, with a heroic performance by the whole side, we won by sixty points to three. The chap with the clipboard was heard to mutter, 'We're Sutton and Epsom. We don't go down by sixty points.' David Halliwell told him that they just had done precisely that. Clipboard man was not best pleased but the league championship was ours.

There was a small matter of a few more games in the calendar, but in the end they were mostly cried off by the opposition. We were champions, and thanks to Danny and the physio I'd been part of the winning team. My back felt awful but the rest of me was just fine.

At the Headquarters of Rugby Union, Twickenham Stadium, home of great international sporting triumphs, a few weeks later a few of us gathered in club ties and blazers for the Surrey Rugby Awards dinner. First, second and third teams from all over the county were gathered around banqueting tables with their club chairmen and presidents. We were there with them. The side that had once been the third-worst side in Surrey was now The Mighty 4s, Champions of the Surrey Foundation League.

We ate well and drank well and waited for our turn as the trophies for some of the leagues around us were handed out. Finally, the master of ceremonies got to our league. We might have been the lowest league but we gave the biggest cheer as Danny Gillespie went up to collect our trophy. Each team had had a suitably celebratory blast of music pumped out over the PA system for their walk up to the stage. Danny's theme tune turned out to be the theme from the classic 1970s TV series and film *Fame*. It couldn't have been cheesier if it had been filmed in Cheddar Gorge, with a camera made out of Gorgonzola. We cheered even louder as he posed for photographs with a couple of the England women's rugby international squad.

Our victory and our championship was nothing whatsoever to do with 'fame'. We were and will remain an utterly unknown, unfamous bit of the sport. The section of the game entirely devoid of paparazzi, WAGS and celebrity. None of the Warlingham 4th XV nor any of the other clubs we played against will be making an appearance on *Strictly Come Dancing* or in the jungle with Ant and Dec. We will instead turn out every weekend, in front of a dozen friends and family if we are lucky, and have a bloody good game of rugby, purely and simply for the pleasure of the game.

We were not going to be picking up a trophy in the glare of press cameras or with the world watching on satellite TV, but our smiles were just as broad and genuine as those of Jonny Wilkinson and Martin Johnson when they picked up the Webb Ellis trophy for winning the Rugby World Cup in Australia. Rugby is just as much our game as theirs and we were champions too.

Chapter 24

A Final Thought

My old psychology lecturer Michael Argyle was right. Rolling around in the mud with a bunch of beer-drinking reprobates has turned out to be an enormously pleasurable experience and has brought a broad smile to an otherwise grumpy face. The causal link between rugby and happiness has been clear as crystal. I wouldn't have had the fun and made the friends without the sport that young William Webb Ellis started when he picked up the ball and ran with it all those years ago.

The only other guaranteed way to stave off depression, according to Professor Argyle, would have been to get religion. The similarities are strong. Just like joining a happy-clappy evangelical church, playing rugby introduced me to a fanatical family with an overwhelming urge to recruit more converts. With mouthguards and shoulder pads, rather than guitars and tambourines, I have found a new faith and become a rugby missionary. Rugby is a great religion, albeit one where we worship beer, mud and thinly controlled acts of violence. With the smell of Deep Heat rather than incense in our nostrils we honour and revere the oval ball.

In spite of its violent reputation, rugby at the lower levels of the game seems to me to be better than many other team sports for spreading happiness and general well-being. Large or small, fast or slow, there is something for everyone as long as you can cope with being ever so slightly splattered into the mud once in a while. Far from being a hot bed of fermenting fascism, rugby is a celebration of diversity where no one is too short, too tall, too fat or too thin to be welcomed into a side. There is a thriving and growing women's game. Wheelchair rugby is a Paralympic sport. Black and white play alongside each other and even the odd Welsh international player has come out, uncontroversially, as gay.

The bruising and the beer might still put off a few but a little fear and the occasional battering, physical and chemical, seems to strengthen the soul. It is said that what doesn't kill you makes you stronger and the odd bust-up on a rugby pitch and booze-up off it certainly did toughen me up a bit. After playing in the Warlingham front row for a few years, managing the media scrum around political party leaders turned into a piece of cake. I felt a lot more confident tackling gatecrashers at my teenage offspring's parties after surviving being gently roughed up by Merton's Ming the Merciless or the odd toothless Gallic prop. As for the boorish beer-drinking culture, well it's there but it's not obligatory. You can partake in large quantities of what Belgian drinkers call 'liquid bread', but you don't have to. A post-match orange juice and lemonade or a hot mug of tea is a perfectly acceptable alternative and no one will necessarily force you to drink your own wee. On the other hand, if you can cope with the odd mind-numbing skinful of foaming ale then there will be plenty of seasoned and experienced drinkers around to see that you get home safely with some, if not all, of your dignity and self-respect intact.

As a nation, we have blown it with our national sport. With its Premier League millionaires, their WAGS, their Bentleys and their unconventional approach to courtship, Association Football has long since sacrificed its claim to be the beautiful game. Football only has space for a very specific sort of sportsman and though many will dream of a glamorous professional career, few will ever make the grade. In search of goals and glory, the super-rich will search all corners of the globe for that elusive star player. No one seems to play football for fun any more, with jumpers for goalposts. Bill Shankly was only half-joking when he said football was more important than life and death. It's about money, and lots of it.

Meanwhile, in almost every living room and on almost every sofa in the country there is a fat bloke who could, and perhaps should, make himself available to his local rugby club. Somewhere there is a captain with fourteen names on his team sheet waiting for a call from a random stranger who wants to give rugby a go. Sedentary sofa man may be useless but he will get a game and no one will mind if he drops the ball or throws it the wrong way, as long as he buys a round afterwards and comes back the following week.

When Britain won the right to stage the Olympics, a great deal was made of the sporting legacy it would leave to the nation. Young people would be inspired to take up sport and we would all become fitter, healthier, happier and more prosperous as a result. Well, I do hope that happens. If some younger people are inspired to pull on some Lycra and run around a track and pit themselves against a stopwatch all will no doubt be well. But I don't think it will be youthful Olympic excellence that inspires grown-ups to discover the joy of team sport. In Olympic terms, the middle-aged can at best aspire to a bit of Boris Johnson-style ceremonial flag waving.

Those of us who hated sport as children will take a lot of persuading to take up any game as grown-ups. Olympic greats will only remind us of our inadequacies and weaknesses. We will ponder on missed opportunities as we snack on pizza and chicken wings in living rooms around the country. It would be far better if a few more of us took a wander down to a nearby rugby club instead. There someone will welcome you with open arms, even if he can't get them round your morbidly obese frame.

Rough-and-ready rugby at the bottom of the Surrey leagues has seen me through a good few of those difficult middle years and as a result I have probably avoided most of the pitfalls of the typical midlife crisis. My midriff is still bigger than it ought to be and the leg muscles that have to cart it around are complaining in the strongest possible terms, but I am still in one piece and life looks good. I'll continue to make myself available and be ready with my kit packed and the opposition's postcode typed into my satnav every Saturday morning during the rugby season. I'm not sure if I'll manage to get selected for the 4ths every week but if Danny 'Anger Management' Gillespie or any other captain picks up the phone and lets me know he is in danger of having to go to uncontested scrums, I will inevitably move heaven and earth to get to whatever rugby pitch he is on.

I am firmly in the middle of my middle age now but, as long as the likes of OAP-bus-pass-wielding Ron Head and the silver scrummager John Glover are still making themselves available, I will invest in a fresh set of boots for the next season. I am now the proud owner of a sky-blue-and-white stripey blazer and may opt to spend some Saturday afternoons on the touchline watching rather than on the pitch playing, but I will always keep a kitbag in the boot of my car just in case.

Have you enjoyed this book?
If so, why not write a review on your favourite website?

Thanks very much for buying this Summersdale book.

www.summersdale.com